A

SOCIOBIOLOGY
COMPENDIUM

A SOCIOBIOLOGY COMPENDIUM

Aphorisms
Sayings
Asides

Del Thiessen

Transaction Publishers
New Brunswick (U.S.A.) and London (U.K.)

Library of Congress Catalog Number: 98-9620
ISBN: 1-56000-372-3
Printed in the United States of America

Library of Congress Cataloging-in-Publication Data

Thiessen, Delbert D.
    A sociobiology compendium : aphorisms, sayings, asides / Del Thiessen.
        p. cm.
    Includes bibliographical references and index.
    ISBN 1-56000-372-3 (cloth : alk. paper)
    1. Aphorisms and apothegms. 2. Human behavior—Quotations, maxims, etc. I. Title.
PN6271.T49   1998
082—dc21   98-9620
                                                                          CIP

Contents

Acknowledgments

Several people contributed to the publication of this book. I am especially indebted to Drs. David Cohen, Devendra Singh, and Joseph Horn, and to Ross DeVere, Ross Speir, Russell Kingston, and P. Matthew Bronstad for critically reading the text and giving me their comments and advice. I dedicate this book to my daughter, Kendell Mayfield.

Del Thiessen

Preface: Our Genetic Beginnings

Sociobiologists—those curmudgeons who believe that culture is a part of our biology—have divined some of our deepest and sometimes darkest motivations. Yoked together in strategies to procreate, the white and black steeds of compassion and hatred, altruism and selfishness, sacrifice and murder, race toward procreation. In a most Darwinian fashion our divided selves lurch this way and that, promoting our advantage, crippling our enemy, and assuring our genetic future.

But it was not sociobiologists who first uncovered our basic desires and fears. They, in a sophisticated manner simply exposed the truths of old. Didn't William Shakespeare speak of our ingrained duality with the comment: "O thou weed, who act so lovely fair, and smell'st so sweet, that the sense aches at thee, would thou hadst never been born!" (*Othello*), and wasn't it Aristotle who deduced our evolutionary and social history when he said: "Every action must be due to one or other of seven causes: chance, nature, compulsion, habit, reasoning, anger, or appetite." So much of what we "know" now, our brethren "knew" then—a never changing flow of aphorisms, sayings, and asides, unrepealed by the science of biology—truth on the tips of many tongues.

To prove my point that knowledge is genetically and historically deep, I've taken the current "scientific findings" in sociobiology and substituted for them the "non-scientific" voices of the ancient and recent past. Traditions, history, and language have all changed since the beginning of our written record, but little else has. Our consciousness today is no different than it was then, and unlikely to change tomorrow. We carry the genes of our past and the same doses of ecstasy and agony. The evolutionary substance of our life speaks to us in the emotional and rational language of our ancestors. We hear it everywhere; we feel it in ourselves.

Introduction: Culture is in Our Evolution

The truth of human nature lies everywhere, in the affirmations of the ancients, the sonnets of Shakespeare, the writings of Cervantes, the poetry of Tennyson, the novels of Hemingway, the music of Beethoven, the muse of Grimm's fairy tales, the biology of Darwin, and the moods of all people. Yes, the truth is there, heaped up beyond comprehension, soaked in the drama of life. Ernest Becker (1973), in his magnificent book, *The Denial of Death*, put it this way: "The man of knowledge in our time is bowed down under a burden he never imagined he would ever have: the overproduction of truth that cannot be consumed."

The burden is not simply the accumulation of knowledge over long periods. We *know* more today than yesterday. But the strange fact is that much of the truth about ourselves has been recognized for hundreds or even thousands of years, reiterated in the thoughts and expressions of great and common minds.

Part of the nature of man is to understand himself. The Greek philosopher and statesman Plato propounded a doctrine of recollection, positing that we possess universal truths that are unfortunately driven from consciousness by the shock of birth. Accordingly, in a vague sort of way we know everything—knowledge that flows back into consciousness with effort and experience.

The idea that we harbor universal knowledge is a recurring theme in philosophy, literature, history, and the arts. Our endless search for the core of our being—life, and especially death—has time and again touched the same cords. Aristotle, working over two thousand years ago, unearthed an encyclopedia of truths about our behavior, many of which swirled through history over and over. Aristotle saw the universality of human behavior that others would view from their own perspective—knowledge on the tip of many tongues. The British novelist Joseph Conrad had no hesitation in expressing the same idea when he said, "The mind of man is capable of anything—because everything is in it, all the past as well as all the future."

Scientists, as well, have more recently expressed similar ideas. Biologist Ralph Berger (1977) put forward the idea that what we know is built into the human organism: "In a certain sense nothing is acquired from the environment and "added" to the brain that was not there before. New connections are not established as a result of experience. In this way the model conforms to Plato's view of learning, that we do not really learn anything new but only "remember" preexisting Forms. Jung's concept of the Collective Unconscious reiterates the same essential idea, since it implies an innate organic basis for the emergence of certain behaviors (or psychological events) that are universal but manifested individually (or culturally) in a variety of symbolic forms."

How could that be? How could we possess universal knowledge? The answers lie in our biology, namely that we are all images of the same evolutionary history, all sharing adaptive mechanisms and strategies, all reflecting the same ecological and social history. What's built into the human mind are the survival and reproductive strategies conserved by natural selection, the drives and cognitive processes that are there because of past adaptations to early environments. Witness how children acquire complex behaviors, such as language and concepts of cause and effect, without specific training. Their minds are prepared to assimilate the crucial features of our environment. As the great developmentalist Jean Piaget understood, children show an unfolding of increasing complexity akin to the revelation of genetic knowledge.

Universal knowledge we seem to understand intuitively; it is knowledge that mirrors the demands of past environments—universal principles that shape our bodies and minds. Our loves, hates, jealousies, ecstasies, concerns for kin, suspicions of strangers, longings for others, fears of death, and all the rest nestle in the brain as strategies of survival and reproduction, common to all, sometimes available to consciousness.

What is Truth?

The difficulty in unveiling our own nature is to sift out the truth from the fiction, the rose from the nettles. For every insight into human behavior, dozens of irrelevant and downright silly propositions are voiced. Aristotle not only spoke the truth about man, he spoke the idiosyncratic notions of his time. He, as all others, could not consistently be insightful beyond his time. At one time Aristotle asserted that, "Every science and every inquiry, and similarly every activity and pursuit, is thought to aim at some good," a proposition with little historical or biological support. But his perspicacity was striking at a different moment when he remarked, "Poetry is something more philosophic and of graver import than history, since its statements are of the nature of universals, whereas those of history are singulars." Utterances obviously reflect the superficialities of a narrow and fanciful focus, or the deep-rooted probing of the inner nature.

How can we tell the difference? What is simply social fluff tied to the concerns of the day, and what cuts through the overlay of cultural vagaries to the very tap-root of existence? Some criteria may help: *truth is found repetitively throughout written and verbal history. It is cast in different languages, forms, and cultural garb, expressed in poetry, literature, art, politics, and business, said independently of previous knowledge, recurring at any time, and eventually gaining consensus and scientific confirmation.* They are universal statements of the human mind.

One criterion of truth emerges above all others, simply the "stab of truth," that quality of feeling that supersedes all others. *Truth is strong, unrelenting, jarring, uncompromising, and seemingly inevitable*—a pain which will not stop. Signals of truth dip deep into the psyche, arousing and evoking emotional reactions: we feel the truth more often than we intellectualize its components. Like other stabs of emotion, we often try to get rid of them with dispatch. That is why, I think, that basic truths do not accumulate as immutable steps toward total understanding. While we search and often feel the truth, we also try not to look at it too closely in the eye. We see it; we blink; we turn the other way, covering ourselves in the cloak of self-deception, calling truth "relative," non-existent, "culturally-determined."

Yes, even self-deception is a form of mental adaptation, in that it reflects a need to obscure facts that are uncomfortable or even dangerous. One might even argue that self-deception is one of the most persuasive attributes of human behavior—it blankets almost everything else.

Life is Tough

Why are some truths so hard to bear? Why do we bury them when they rear their heads? The reasons vary, I suppose, but the most general answer is that we prefer not to know. Non-defensive truth, what we for sake of convenience will simply call truth, is a demon that cuts to the quick, destroying illusions as it goes—illusions of superiority, power, uniqueness, goodness, equality, and, yes, immortality. We battle truth as we would an invasive microorganism.

Illusions support and guide our existence. They cover our weaknesses, camouflage our ambitions, rationalize our most basic behaviors, smooth our interactions with others, and lead us to reproduction. Illusions are aces in a game of survival. If we can deceive ourselves about the most important things, we hang on to our integrity and gain advantages over others. Life moves on the rails of deception, laid deeply in the sands of time, coded into the cellular DNA.

In short, illusions of life are essential for individual survival and reproduction. They appear as evolutionary adaptations as strong as any— essential strategies that make the absurd reasonable, the impossible possible, and the unbearable bearable. Like other survival strategies they swirl in our unconsciousness, pulling back other truths and making themselves plausible. In this game the truth seeker breaks through the illusory shield and pulls knowledge forward. Simultaneously, the truth seeker sees illusions as another form of truth, veiled and intangible, but crucial to existence.

Thus, we stand in conflict of seeking truths built into the fabric of the central nervous system, while also straining against the illusions that force us to resist those truths. From time immemorial, courageous individuals flirted with both, in the end trading personal comfort for philosophical and scientific revelations.

The Place of Science

Touching the truth within us is not science, but it is the stone from which science springs. Albert Einstein reminded us that, "The whole of science is nothing more than a refinement of common thinking." Einstein was referring to the *logic* of science, not the outcome, although he was acutely aware that the fundamental nature of the universe reflects both its history and our innate ability to recognize truth when we see it.

Francis Crick, the codiscoverer of the double-helix structure of DNA, was brash enough to declare that, "We have discovered the secret of life." It was a monumental discovery—the literal unveiling of the genetic structure of life—but it was not *the* secret of life. Charles Darwin and Alfred Russell Wallace, the cofounders of the theory of natural selection, were arguably closer, as exemplified by Darwin's comment that, "We tend to pass on those traits to the next generation that enhance reproduction." This simple statement implies a universe of competition, differential survival, reproductive drives, and genetic transmission.

Ultimately there is something simple, graceful, and beautiful about revealed truth. The famous nuclear physicist Werner Heisenberg expressed this idea in a conversation with Albert Einstein: "If nature leads us to mathematical forms of great simplicity and beauty—by forms I am referring to coherent systems of hypotheses, axioms, etc.—to forms that no one has previously encountered, we cannot help thinking that they are "true," that they reveal a genuine feature of nature... You must have felt this too: The almost frightening simplicity and wholeness of the relationships which nature suddenly spreads out before us and for which none of us was in the least prepared." For Heisenberg the simple is the seal of truth, beauty its splendor, self-revelation its messenger.

But scientists receive too much of the credit. What we fail to recognize is that the truth about the universe, about human behavior—its origins, its destiny—is within us all. We reflect the nature of our evolution, spun out over billions of years, ringing true to the principles of the physical universe, mirroring all common solutions, bearing the load of successful survival and reproduction. Our lives are destiny seen backward—a chilling scenario of past conquests and deep crimes. It is all there, all we will ever know, all that matters. The reflection of universal principles are imprinted in the DNA helix—the code for successful living, run out through Darwinian rules, headed for nothing in particular.

Our evolutionary history is the repository of self-knowledge, and also our constraint. We see through the genetic visions of the past, but remain blind to the future. Science can express and clarify knowledge, but it can't create new knowledge that in some form is not already there. We can build devices to extend our sensory and perceptual reach, but we can't go beyond our psychological and cognitive limitations. In some metaphorical sense, we view the world through a narrow tube, limited entirely by our animalistic nature. We know ourselves only from the perspective of evolution past. But we do know that, at least, and have for ages. What science can readily do is better describe our nature, opening the window to even deeper levels of truth.

The skeptic must answer the question, what has science told us about life that has not already been gleaned by Aristotle, Confucius, Buddha, Jesus, Shakespeare, and countless others? The deep-structured knowledge sprouts fourth repeatedly, there to be harvested and expressed harmoniously by scientists.

1

The Nature of Man

Biologists have long believed in the similarities between humans and other species. Charles Darwin (1871) made the case by arguing that all animals are linked by their evolutionary history: "Every evolutionist will admit that the five great vertebrate classes, namely, mammals, birds, reptiles, amphibians, and fishes, are descended from some one prototype; for they have much in common, especially during their embryonic state. As the class of fishes is the most lowly organized, and appeared before the others, we may conclude that all the members of the vertebrate kingdom are derived from some fishlike animal." Indeed, the ties are strong. For example, humans and chimpanzees overlap in about 98.4 percent of their DNA (Sarich & Wilson, 1967), sharing similar physical traits, physiologies, and behaviors. We did not evolve directly from chimpanzee, but both we and the chimpanzee have a common ancestor that goes back about 10 to 15 million years (Johanson, Johanson & Edgar, 1994).

Our history of evolution ensures that we reflect our primate heritage. As with other contemporaneous primates we exist because our nature was honed by natural selection for traits that facilitated survival and reproduction. All else failed, leaving us with a hard core of evolved adaptations. We carry these adaptations everywhere—traits and strategies designed for past environments, but hardly for today's complex world (Tooby & Cosmides, 1992). Anthropologist Donald Symons (1992) summarized the argument by saying that "Natural selection takes hundreds or thousands of gene changes to fashion any *complex* adaptation. The brain/mind mechanisms that constitute human nature were shaped by selection over vast periods of time in environments different in many important respects from our own, and it is to these ancient environments that human nature is adapted."

Living with Limitations

The adaptations of yesterday are the constraints of today. As a result, our alternatives are limited. All we can do is apply yesterday's designs to today's problems. Like a Model-A Ford, built for the needs of past generations, the Model-A is limited in today's environment. The Model-A can never become a 1996 Mercedes, no more than *Homo sapiens* can change into anything else. A Model-A can be painted, or in other ways fixed up, but it does not become something different. It survives and replicates, or goes extinct.

Whether we like it or not, we ride the waves of past evolution, fixed in our characteristics, constrained in our abilities, stuck with what we are. Individuals differ, passing these differences on to their children, but the variations only highlight the common traits around which differences swirl. Fundamentally, we strive for reproduction using adaptations of the past, playing out our selfish manner programmed by natural selection (Dawkins, 1976). We get along with others either because we share genes, as with kin, or because individuals learn to reciprocate for mutual benefit. Often our behaviors appear truly altruistic, but it all seems aimed to ensure personal advantage and gene perpetuation. I believe that it was sociobiologist Edward O. Wilson (1975) who said, "Scratch an altruist and watch a hypocrite bleed."

Surprisingly, most of what we are we deny. Our nature is simply too harsh, riddled with paradoxes, empty of hope, destined for destruction. The environment is indifferent to our success or failure—it is simply there. Biologists have not dealt well with the illusory veils of our lives, especially those that cover our inadequacies and hide our ultimate fate. Some have tried (Lopreato, 1984), but few have accepted the tough reality of natural selection. The cellular biologist William Provine (see Liles, 1994) spells out the implications:

- There are no gods or purposive forces in nature.
- There are no inherent moral or ethical laws to guide human society.
- Human beings are complex machines that become ethical beings by way of heredity and environmental influences...
- There is no free will in the traditional sense of being able to make uncoerced and unpredictable choices.
- When we die, we die—finally and completely and forever.

In dealing with hard realities we immerse ourselves in religion and self-deception. According to the sociologist Ernest Becker (1973), we build our gods, create heroes, and repress our anxieties as "...an attempt to attain 'an immunity bath' from the greatest evil: death and the dread of it. All historical religions addressed themselves to this same problem of how to bear the end of life. Religions like Hinduism and Buddhism performed the ingenious trick of pretending not to want to be reborn, which is a sort of negative magic: claiming not to want what you really want most. When philosophy took over from religion it also took over religion's central problem, and death became the real 'muse of philosophy' from its beginnings in Greece right through Heidegger and modern existentialism." In these matters biologists search for the mechanisms controlling our lives; intellectuals contemplate our origin.

Bitter-Sweet Destiny

The Animal Within Us

I imagine that if we were the only mammals on earth we might overlook our links to other animals. As we know, we do have close relatives among primates and our links have never been ignored—embarrassed though we may be.

Whenever you observe an animal closely, you feel as if a human being sitting inside were making fun of you.

Elias Canetti
Austrian novelist

I find it valid to understand man as an animal before I am prepared to know him as a man.

John Steinbeck
American writer

We are very slightly changed from the semi-apes who ranged India's prehistories clay.

Rudyard Kipling
British writer

All nature's creatures join to express nature's purpose. Somewhere in their mounting and mating, ratting and butting is the very secret of nature itself.

Graham Swift
British novelist

How like us is that ugly brute, the ape!

Ennius
Roman poet

Cats and monkeys, monkeys and cats—all human life is there.

Henry James
American novelist

In a few generations more, there will probably be no room at all allowed for animals on the earth: no need of them, no toleration of them. An immense agony will have then ceased, but with it there will also have passed away the last smile of the world's youth.

Ouida (Marie Louise de la Ramée)
British novelist

Knowledge Comes from Within

The evidence that fundamental knowledge is harbored in everyone comes from many quarters. Knowledge shines through irrationality, philosophical discourse, and personal observation. It comes without warning, hidden within—nothing specifically learned.

Nature has planted in our minds an insatiable longing to see the truth.

Cicero
Roman orator

Do you really believe that the sciences would ever have originated and grown if the way had not been prepared by magicians, alchemists, astrologers and witches whose promises and pretensions first had to create a thirst, a hunger, a taste for *hidden* and *forbidden* powers? Indeed, infinitely more had to be *promised* than could ever be fulfilled in order that anything at all might be fulfilled in the realms of knowledge.

Friedrich Nietzsche
German philosopher

It needs no dictionary of quotations to remind me that the eyes are the windows of the soul.

Sir Max Beerbohm
British essayist

Art and religion first; then philosophy; lastly science. That is the order of the great subjects of life, that's their order of importance.

Muriel Spark
British novelist

Science is for those who learn; poetry, for those who know.

Joseph Roux
French priest

None of the great discoveries was made by a 'specialist' or a 'researcher.'

Martin H. Fischer
A "Fischerism"

Sciences may be learned by rote, but wisdom not.

Laurence Sterne

A thought is often original, though you have uttered it a hundred times.

Oliver Wendell Holmes
American writer

The essence of knowledge (the *Purusha*) being unchangeable, when the mind takes its form, it becomes conscious.

The Yoga Aphorisms of Patanjali

Knowledge is what we get when an observer, preferably a scientifically trained observer, provides us with a copy of reality that we can all recognize.

Christopher Lasch
American historian

...that is what learning is. You suddenly understand something you've understood all your life, but in a new way.

Doris Lessing
British novelist

Thus absolute truth is indestructible. Being indestructible, it is eternal. Being eternal, it is self-existent. Being self-existent, it is infinite. Being infinite, it is vast and deep. Being vast and deep, it is transcendental and intelligent.

Confucius
Chinese philosopher

The things we know best are the things we haven't been taught.

Luc, Marquis de Vauvenargues
French moralist

I believe the souls of five hundred Sir Isaac Newtons would go to the making up of a Shakespeare or a Milton.

Samuel Taylor Coleridge
English poet

Facts Count, but Little

We constantly face facts, but they only have life through intuition and judgment. These processes are the nature by which we tap into universal knowledge.

Facts are not science—as the dictionary is not literature.

Martin H. Fischer
A "Fischerism"

Facts are ventriloquist's dummies. Sitting on a wise man's knee they may be made to utter words of wisdom; elsewhere they say nothing or talk nonsense.

Aldous Huxley
British novelist

Don't despise empiric truth. Lots of things work in practice for which the laboratory has never found truth.

Martin H. Fischer
A "Fischerism"

Obviously the facts are never just coming at you but are incorporated by an imagination that is formed by your previous experience. Memories of the past are not memories of facts but memories of your imaginings of the facts.

Philip Roth
American novelist

Truth Steps Forth as Beauty

Poets, novelists, and others have long been intrigued by the relations between truth and beauty. Perhaps because truths express the basic principles of life, they often seem simple and beautiful.

What the imagination seizes as beauty must be truth.

John Keats
English poet

You know very well that unless you're a scientist, it's much more important for a theory to be shapely, than for it to be true.

Christopher Hampton
British writer

We ascribe beauty to that which is simple; which has no superfluous parts; which exactly answers its end; which stands related to all things; which is the mean of many extremes.

Ralph Waldo Emerson
American poet

'Beauty is truth, truth beauty,' that is all ye know on earth, and all ye need to know.

John Keats
English poet

There are two kinds of truth; the truth that lights the way and the truth that warms the heart. The first of these is science, and the second is art... Without art science would be as useless as a pair of high forceps in the hands of a plumber. Without science art would become a crude mess of folklore and emotional quackery.

Raymond Chandler
American novelist

Universal Truths are Always There

Man is an evolutionary experiment, initiated with the first single cell and extending through 3.5 billion years. Each new successful ancestor retained the rules of life that permitted it to survive and reproduce. Multiplied across innumerable species and thousands of generations, truths become part of the general protoplasm. We, a late benefactor of that accumulative knowledge, carry much of the universe within us.

The thing that hath been, it is that which shall be; and that which is done is that which shall be done: and there is no new thing under the sun.

Bible: Ecclesiastes 1: 7-9

Nothing is said nowadays that has not been said before.

Terence (Publius Terentius Afer)
Roman playwright

There are no new truths, but only truths that have not been recognized by those who have perceived them without noticing. A truth is something that everybody can be shown to know and to have known, as people say, all along.

Mary McCarthy
American author and critic

Every man carries the entire form of human condition.

Michel de Montaigne
French moralist

It is universally acknowledged, that there is a great uniformity among the actions of men, in all nations and ages, and that human nature remains still the same, in its principles and operations. The same motives always produce the same actions: The same events follow from the same causes.

David Hume
Scottish philosopher

We are born believing. A man bears beliefs as a tree bears apples.

Ralph Waldo Emerson
American poet

We never remark any passion or principle in others, of which, in some degree or other, we may not find a parallel in ourselves.

David Hume
Scottish philosopher

We must turn to nature itself, to the observations of the body in health and disease to learn the truth.

Hippocrates
Greek physician

He was naturally learned; he needed not the spectacles of books to read nature; he looked inwards and found her there.

John Dryden
English poet

He first wrote, wine is the strongest. The second wrote, the king is strongest. The third wrote, women are strongest: but above all things truth beareth away the victory.

Apocrypha
1 Esdras 3: 10-2

Truth has no special time of its own. It's hour is now—always.

Albert Schweitzer
French physician

Truth is on the march; nothing can stop it.

Emile Zola
French novelist

Deception and Reluctance to See Truth

The paradox of life is that we live with truths *and* deceptions, both evolving throughout history. One hangs on the other, as if the reach for truth stimulates the flow of anti-truth—a continuous battle in the mind.

Truth may not depart from human nature. If what is regarded as truth departs from human nature, it may not be regarded as truth.

Confucius
Chinese philosopher

It is not because the truth is too difficult to see that we make mistakes. It may even lie on the surface; but we make mistakes because the easiest and most comfortable course for us is to seek insight where it accords with our emotions—especially selfish ones.

Alexander Solzhenitsyn
Russian novelist

As a rule people are afraid of truth. Each truth we discover in nature or social life destroys the crutches on which we need to lean.

Ernst Toller
German playwright

Laws which prescribe what everyone must believe, and forbid men to say or write anything against this or that opinion, are often passed to gratify, or rather, to appease the anger of those who cannot abide independent minds.

Benedict Spinoza
Dutch philosopher

"...for the habitual truth-teller and truth-seeker, indeed the world · has very little liking...Even today, with the scientific passions becoming familiar in the world, the general view of such fellows is highly unfavorable. The typical scientist, the typical critic of institutions, the typical truth-seeker in every field is held under suspicion by the great majority of men, and variously beset by posses of relentless foes... The men the American people admire most extravagantly are the most daring liars... [those] with an extraordinary genius for swathing the bitter facts of life in bandages of soft illusion."

H. L. Mencken
American Journalist

What was once thought can never be unthought.

Friedrich Dürrenmatt
Swiss writer

Even when poetry has a meaning, as it usually has, it may be inadvisable to draw it out...perfect understanding will sometimes almost extinguish pleasure.

A.E. Housman
British poet

We have to believe in free will. We've got no choice.

Isaac Bashevis Singer
American writer

I drink not from mere joy in wine nor to scoff at faith—no, only to forget myself for a moment, that only do I want of intoxication, that alone.

Omar Khayyám (Edward Fitzgerald, trans.)
Persian poet

Take stock of those around you and you will...hear them talking in precise terms about themselves and their surroundings, which would seem to point to them having ideas on the matter. But start to analyze those ideas and you will find that they hardly reflect in any way the reality to which they appear to refer, and if you go deeper you will discover that there is not even an attempt to adjust the ideas to this reality. Quite the contrary: through these notions the individual is trying to cut off any personal vision of reality, of his own very life. For life is at the start a chaos in which one is lost. The individual suspects this, but he is frightened at finding himself face to face with this terrible reality, and tries to cover it over with a curtain of fantasy, where everything is clear. It does not worry him that his "ideas" are not true, he uses them as trenches for the defense of his existence, as scarecrows to frighten away reality.

José Ortega y Gasset
Spanish philosopher

The Inevitability of Nature's Stamp

We fight it, but everywhere we find that our fate is deep within our evolutionary history. Some say that our destiny is thereby fixed.

From our earliest hour we have been taught that the thought of the heart, the shaping of the rain-cloud, the amount of wool that grows on a sheep's back, the length of a drought, and the growing of the corn, depend on nothing that moves immutable, at the heart of all things; but on the changeable will of a changeable being, whom our prayers can alter. To us, from the beginning, Nature has been but a poor plastic thing, to be toyed with this way or that, as man happens to please his deity or not; to go to church or not; to say his prayers right or not; to travel on Sunday or not. Was it possible for us in an instant to see Nature as she is—the flowing vestment of unchanging reality.

Olive Schreiner
South African writer

The eye—it cannot choose but see; we cannot bid the ear be still; our bodies feel, where're they be, against or with our will.

William Wordsworth
English poet

Man the machine—man the impersonal engine. Whatsoever a man is, is due to his *maker,* and to the *influence* brought to bear upon it by his heredities. He is moved, corrected, COMMANDED, by exterior influences—solely. He *originates* nothing, not even a thought.

Samuel Langhorne Clemens (Mark Twain)
American writer

Even God cannot make two times two not make four.

Hugo Grotius
Dutch theologian

Nothing under the sun is accidental.

Gotthold Ephraim Lessing
German critic

Every why hath a wherefore.

William Shakespeare
English playwright

Not even the gods can undo what has been done.

Plutarch
Greek historian

Home life is no more natural to us than a cage is to a cockatoo.

George Bernard Shaw
Irish dramatist

You can drive out nature with a pitchfork, and she will always return.

Horace
Roman poet

It is absolutely impossible to transcend the laws of nature. What can change in historically different circumstances is only the form in which these laws expose themselves.

Karl Marx
German social philosopher

Nature to be commanded, must be obeyed.

Francis Bacon
British philosopher

Whatever may happen to you was prepared for you from all eternity; and the implication of causes was from eternity spinning the thread of your being.

Marcus Aurelius
Roman emperor

Nature admits no lie.

Thomas Carlyle
Scottish historian

Nature never breaks her own laws.

Leonardo da Vinci
Florentine painter

No truth is more certain than this, that all that happens, be it small or great, happens with absolute necessity.

Arthur Schopenhauer
German philosopher

Whatever is, is right.

Democritus
Greek philosopher

The law of nature is so unalterable that it cannot be changed by God Himself.

Hugo Grotius
Dutch theologian

The mind of man is capable of anything—because everything is in it, all the past as well as all the future.

Joseph Conrad
British novelist

It is written in the *Analects* of Confucius "The Master said, Heaven does not speak."

Attributed to Confucius

Nature is an endless combination and repetition of a very few laws. She hums the old well-known air through innumerable variations.

Ralph Waldo Emerson
American poet

Man is a microcosm, or a little world, because he is an extract from all the stars and planets of the whole firmament, from the earth and the elements; and so he is their quintessence.

Philipus Aureolus Paracelsus
German physician

The Power of Evolution

Our genetic history, that is, our evolutionary history, powerfully locked us into our humanism. We are determined by our past and by the physiological equipment that facilitated our survival. We are born; we feed; we reproduce. We have long understood this.

The tide of evolution carries everything before it, thoughts no less than bodies, and persons no less than nations.

George Santayana
American philosopher

The survival of the fittest, which I have here sought to express in mechanical terms, is that which Mr. Darwin called "natural selection," or the preservation of favored races in the struggle for life.

Herbert Spencer
British philosopher

Nature is entirely neutral; she submits to him who most energetically and resolutely assails her. She grants her rewards to the fittest.

William Graham Sumner
American economist

Biologically the species is the accumulation of the experiments of all its successful individuals since the beginning.

H. G. Wells
British Author

If a single cell, under appropriate conditions, becomes a man in the space of a few years, there can surely be no difficulty in understanding how, under appropriate conditions, a cell may, in the course of untold millions of years, give origin to the human race.

Herbert Spencer
British philosopher

When you're young, all evolution lies before you, every road is open to you, and at the same time you can enjoy the fact of being there on the rock, flat mollusk-pulp, damp and happy. If you compare yourself with the limitations that come afterwards, if you think of how having one form excludes other forms, of the monotonous routine where you finally feel trapped, well, I don't mind saying life was beautiful in those days.

Italo Calvino
Italian writer

Nothing exists per se except atoms and the void.

Lucretius
Roman poet

What we feel and think and are is to a great extent determined by the state of our ductless glands and viscera.

Aldous Huxley
British novelist

Of course, Behaviorism "works." So does torture. Give me a no-nonsense, down-to-earth behaviorist, a few drugs, and simple electrical appliances, and in six months I will have him reciting the Athanasian Creed in public.

W. H. Auden
English poet

In nature there are neither rewards nor punishments—there are consequences.

Robert G. Ingersoll
American lawyer

The whole of nature is a conjugation of the verb to eat, in the active and the passive.

Dean William Ralph Inge
British churchman

It is an old maxim of mine that when you have excluded the impossible, whatever remains, however improbable, must be the truth.

Arthur Conan Doyle
British writer

There never comes a point where a theory can be said to be true. The most that one can claim for any theory is that it has shared the successes of all its rivals and that it has passed at least one test which they have failed.

A. J. Ayer
British philosopher

Theories that go counter to the facts of human nature are foredoomed.

Edith Hamilton
American classical scholar

The moral virtues, then, are produced in us neither by nature nor against nature. Nature, indeed, prepares in us the ground for their reception, but their complete formation is the product of habit.

Aristotle
Greek philosopher

It is only shallow people who do not judge by appearances. The true mystery of the world is the visible, not the invisible.

Oscar Wilde
Irish playwright

Life's but a walking shadow, a poor player that struts and frets his hour upon the stage and then is heard no more. It is a tale told by an idiot, full of sound and fury, signifying nothing.

William Shakespeare
English playwright

Inherited Traits and Deep Tendencies

Our behavioral nature is reflected in the structure of our bodies, in our faces, and even our movements. Writers have known for centuries that our characteristics are transmitted across generations. Only recently have we discovered that our nature is programmed in our cellular DNA.

Do you see this egg? With this you can topple every theological theory, every church or temple in the world.

Denis Diderot
French philosopher

A hen is only an egg's way of making another egg.

Samuel Butler
English writer

Like father, like son.

Proverb

The generations of living things pass in a short time, and like runners hand on the torch of life.

Lucretius
Roman philosopher

The child is father of the man.

William Wordsworth
English poet

Men are made by nature unequal. It is vain, therefore, to treat them as if they were equal.

J. A. Froude
British historian

Equality may perhaps be a right, but no power on earth can ever turn it into a fact.

Honoré de Balzac
French novelist

By law of nature thou art bound to breed,
That thine may live when thou thyself art dead;
And so, in spite of death, thou dost survive,
In that thy likeness still is left alive.

William Shakespeare
English playwright

A man finds room in the few square inches of the face for the traits of all his ancestors; for the expression of all his history, and his wants.

Ralph Waldo Emerson
American poet

The modifications of Nature, in one way or other produced, are inheritable.

Herbert Spencer
British philosopher

Does Nature care in the least whether we evolve or not? Her instincts are for the gratification of hunger and sex, the destruction of rivals, and the protection of offspring. What monster first slipped in the idea of progress?

Cyril Connolly
English essayist

Whatever a man may happen to turn, whatever a man may undertake, he will always end up by returning to that path which nature has marked out for him.

Johann Wolfgang von Goethe
German poet

The Selfish Gene

Natural selection exaggerates individual traits that are associated with successful reproduction. Selfishness, in particular, is a trait for successful reproduction, known over the ages, obvious to many.

I am done with the monster of "We," the word of serfdom, of plunder, of misery, falsehood and shame. And now I see the free face of god, and I raise this god over the earth, this god whom men have sought since men came into being, this god who will grant them joy and peace and pride. This god, this one word: "I."

Ayn Rand
American writer

It is not from the benevolence of the butcher, or the baker, that we expect our dinner, but from their regard to their own interest. We address ourselves, not to their humanity but to their self-love, and never talk to them of our necessities but of their advantages.

Adam Smith
Scottish economist

From none but self expect applause, he noblest lives and noblest dies, who makes and keeps his self-made laws.

Sir Richard Burton
British statesman

Self-love is the greatest of all flatterers.

Francois, Duc de la Rochefoucauld
French writer

The fact is that a man who wants to act virtuously in every way necessarily comes to grief among so many who are not virtuous.

Niccolò Machiavelli
Italian statesman

Fear is an emotion indispensable for survival.

Hannah Arendt
American philosopher

The present is never our goal: the past and present are our means: the future alone is our goal. Thus, we never live but we hope to live; and always hoping to be happy, it is inevitable that we will never be so.

Blaise Pascal
French philosopher

The endeavor for self-preservation is the primary and only foundation of virtue.

Benedict Spinoza
Dutch philosopher

There is no such thing as "natural law": this expression is nothing but old nonsense. Prior to laws, what is natural is only the strength of the lion, or the need of the creature suffering from hunger or cold, in short, need.

Stendhal (Marie-Henri Beyle)
French writer

Nature...is nothing but the inner voice of self-interest.

Charles Baudelaire
French poet

The hair grows old with aging years; the teeth grow old, the eyes and ears. But while the aging seasons speed, one thing is young forever—greed.

The Panchatantra
Translated by Arthur W. Ryder

Narcissus does not fall in love with his reflection because it is beautiful, but because it is *his*. If it were his beauty that enthralled him, he would be set free in a few years by its fading.

W. H. Auden
English poet

Rich men deal gifts, expecting in return twenty for one?

William Shakespeare
English playwright

The punters know that the horse named Morality rarely gets past the post, whereas the nag named Self-Interest always runs a good race.

Gough Whitlam
Australian labor politician

I have never grown out of the infantile belief that the universe was made for me to suck.

Aleister Crowley
British author

Everyone believes that what suits him is the right thing to do.

Johann Wolfgang von Goethe
German poet

Desire is the very essence of man.

Benedict Spinoza
Dutch philosopher

There are only two forces that unite men—fear and interest.

Napoleon Bonaparte
French general and emperor

When you don't have any money, the problem is food. When you have money, it's sex. When you have both, it's health. If everything is simply jake, then you're frightened of death.

J. P. Donleavy
American writer

Instinct. When the house burns one forgets even lunch. Yes, but one eats it later in the ashes.

Friedrich Nietzsche
German philosopher

Be selfish. Nothing else makes the human race predictable.

John Ciardi
American poet

Remember how often you have postponed minding your interest, and let slip those opportunities the gods have given you. It is now high time to consider what sort of world you are part of, and from what kind of governor of it you are descended; that you have a set period assigned you to act in, and unless you improve it to brighten and compose your thoughts, it will quickly run off with you, and be lost beyond recovery.

Marcus Aurelius
Roman emperor

Death as the Great Motivator

Death is always in the mix, always denied, dreaded, and feared. Yet, unknown to all but the most astute philosophers, our characteristics are often immortal, escaping the grave as they pass on to our children. More accurately, the genes are the source of our immortality, not our bodies. Bodies only project the genes from one generation to the next.

I believe that the struggle against death, the unconditional and self-willed determination to live, is the motive power behind the lives and activities of all outstanding men.

Herman Hesse
German novelist

He who pretends to look on death without fear lies. All men are afraid of dying, this is the great law of sentient beings, without which the entire human species would soon be destroyed.

Jean-Jacques Rousseau
French philosopher

Down, down, down into the darkness of the grave gently they go, the beautiful, the tender, the kind; quietly they go, the intelligent, the witty, the brave. I know. But I do not approve. And I am not resigned.

Edna St. Vincent Millay
American poet

A time will come when this Universe and Nature itself will be extinguished... Of the entire world and of the vicissitudes and calamities of all created things there will remain not a single trace, but a naked silence and a most profound stillness will fill the immensity of space. And so before ever it has uttered or understood, this admirable and fearful secret of universal existence will be obliterated and lost.

Giacomo Leopardi
Italian poet

All the world's a stage, and all the men and women merely players; they have their exits and their entrances, and one man in his time plays many parts, his acts being seven ages.

William Shakespeare
English playwright

'Tis all a Chequer-board of Nights and Days where Destiny with Men for Pieces plays; Hither and thither moves, and mates, and slays, And one by one back in the Closet lays.

Omar Khayyám (Edward Fitzgerald, trans.)
Persian poet

It is natural to die as to be born; and to a little infant, perhaps, the one is as painful as the other.

Francis Bacon
English philosopher

There is death in the pot.

Bible: 2 Kings 4: 40

Birth, copulation, and death. That's all the facts when you come to brass tacks.

T. S. Eliot
Anglo-American poet

The worst is death, and death will have its day.

William Shakespeare
English playwright

Cut it short! On doomsday 'twon't be worth a farthing!'

Johann Wolfgang von Goethe
German poet

Our little systems have their day; they have their day and cease to be.

Alfred Lord Tennyson
English poet

The major problem of our time is decay of the belief in personal immortality.

George Orwell
British writer

Hope is the worst of evils, for it prolongs the torments of man.

Friedrich Nietzsche
German philosopher

And yet, hope pursues me, encircles me, bites me; like a dying wolf tightening his grip for the last time.

Federico García Lorca
Spanish poet

Let's not have a sniffle, lets have a bloody good cry. And always remember the longer you live, the sooner you'll bloody well die!

Irish ballad

Do not go gentle into that good night, old age should burn and rave at close of day; rage, rage, against the dying of the light.

Dylan Thomas
Welsh poet

We sense the animal within us, linking our moods and intellect with other species. It becomes unavoidable to think that we represent a major product of biological evolution. Our behaviors were formed from earlier species—we have an inevitability that is animal-like in nature.

Man has always known the two deep secrets of life: (1) the truth of our existence is deep within our psyche—always there, sometimes available to consciousness, and (2) the truth about ourselves is difficult to live with—we deceive ourselves at every turn. When a truth about our nature does emerge it is often simple, traumatic, beautiful, and irresistible. Each of us share the same secrets, characterizing our species, our nature. Unlocking these secrets presents the stuff on which biology rests and with which science progresses.

Our ancestors survived because of their selfishness and dedication to reproduction. We, derived from our selfish ancestors, carry the same strategies. From the Grecian philosophers to contemporary Ayn Rand we have understood this and adapted.

We have adapted less to our obvious mortality. Death robs us of contentment and motivates most of our thoughts and behaviors. Poets and the like point this out repeatedly, forcing us to confront our destiny. Biology has only lately begun to understand the implications of our fear of death, and strives to incorporate these into our scientific theories. Pointed out by scientists, we do have genetic immortality, passing on our genes and traits to our children. Genes link us to our ancestors and our future.

2

Romantic Love, Passion, and
the Price of Reproduction

Love makes the world go 'round, so the proverb goes. Perhaps, if love includes sex and reproduction. Certainly love is a strong drive, and probably universal. Anthropologist Helen Fisher (1992) indicates that at least 87 percent of the world's cultures have a concept of romantic or passionate love. William Jankowiak and Edward Fischer (1992) found that in 166 hunting, foraging, and agricultural societies only one had no apparent evidence for passionate love. Perhaps it isn't always romantic love or passion in the Western sense, but lust, heterosexual bonding, and commitment are nearly universal. Whatever it is, heterosexual relations are often passionate, irrational, and extreme. It depends.

The way people view each other is frankly biological. Biologist Robert Trivers (1972) postulated that males and females pursue and reject each other according to their needs to procreate. These needs differ in males and females, echoing past evolutionary designs for successful reproduction. Males tend to be more lustful, following an evolutionary dictum of maximal sex with minimal investment. Females, in contrast, are more cautious and reticent, having a higher investment in each reproductive act. Unlike males, females produce fewer and more nutritive gametes, undergo long periods of gestation, and engage in lactation and long periods of infant care. As a result, females attempt to choose males with "good" DNA, or those who will contribute to the welfare of her and her offspring. Males more often compete with other males for access to females, and females are less willing to engage in promiscuous sex. The game of love is played out on the backs of these differential investments: male and female attitudes, emotions, and behaviors swirl around these differences.

The consequences of these sexual differences spring forth in many forms. Evolutionary psychologist David Buss (1994) emphasizes that males and females seek different things from each other. Among 37 cultures investigated around the world adult males are overwhelmingly interested in female youth and beauty—indices of reproductive "value". Females, with heavier reproductive investments, are interested in older "proven" males who are ambitious and socially capable of funneling resources into the females' investment in offspring. Put in other words, males are oriented toward attractive females, competing heavily for access to things females desire; females prefer males of quality—males with resource capabilities, males with "good" genes.

In keeping with these notions, Daniel Pérusse (1993) showed that Canadian men with good incomes acquire more sexual partners than do men with poor incomes, precisely because females prefer them. Worldwide, men with resources reproduce more than other men (Betzig, 1986). Even among other primate and non-primate species, social domi-nance and resource capabilities translate into high reproductive levels (Ellis, 1995).

Among humans love often leads to marriage and children. Over 90 percent of all American men and women marry, with women bearing an average of 1.8 children that survive to maturity. Marriage is univer-sal. Many of these marriages don't last over four to seven years, espe-cially if reproduction is not successful. In a study of 160 societies anthropologist Laura Betzig (1989) rank orders the following reasons for dissolution of a marriage:

- Philandering, particularly by the female
- Sterility and barrenness
- Cruelty, especially by the husband
- Personality characteristics, such as bad temper, nonsupport, neglect

Jealousy may be a primary reason for divorce, but having a different basis in males and females. Males, with their concern for paternity, express jealousy about the sexual behaviors of females; females are likely to show jealousy about the distribution of males' resources (Buss, Larsen, Westen & Semmelbroth, 1992).

Biologists conclude that males and females differ in a number of traits that surround unequal investments in offspring. The nature of the female is crucial in the evolutionary game of reproduction, as she is the limiting source for reproduction and, more than the male, must time her reproduction with environmental conditions that support her efforts. As I once suggested (Thiessen, 1993), "There is a correlation between the [sexual] variation expressed and female potential—females tend to shift dramatically from sexual inhibition to sexual expression. Females apparently track the quality of the environment and link their sexuality to reproductive opportunities. Successful male reproduction depends less on quality environments and more on the availability of females. In short, females track the environment; males track the females."

In the larger picture of reproduction men and women use signs of beauty as measures of reproductive potential. Males like women with "hour-glass" physiques, as these dimensions correlate with health, hormonal status, and the ability to ovulate (Singh, 1993). They also seek signs of youth, such as juvenile traits—signs that correlate with a long reproductive life (Johnston & Franklin, 1993; Thornhill, 1993). Both sexes want health and vigor in their mates, and they also prefer mates who are similar in genetic, physical, and psychological traits (Rushton, 1995; Thiessen & Gregg, 1980). Presumably, couples who share basic qualities are more compatible and more likely to reproduce.

Like the Yin and Yang of Oriental philosophy, if males and females play their evolutionary cards successfully the two fit together and the next generation is served. Sexual strategies differ, but they are aimed at successful reproduction. That's the message of evolution; that's the message given to us by those who have long sought the truth of nature.

Love and Reproduction

Love and Possession

Love may be a delusion of sorts, in that it is a powerful screen for the transmission of genes, and it may take a multitude of forms depending on culture, but the fact is that what we normally think love is, it serves the genotype well. We fall in love, enveloping us in passion, lusts, and beauties. Love of that intensity rarely lasts longer than necessary to reproduce. But, ah, what a high!

As a perfume doth remain in the folds where it hath lain, so the thought of you, remaining deeply folded in my brain, will not leave me; all things leave me: you remain.

Arthur Symons
British poet

Say, that the sense of feeling were bereft me, and that I could not see, nor hear, nor touch, and nothing but the very smell were left me. Yet would my love to thee be still as much; for from the stillitory of thy face excelling comes breath perfumed that breedeth love by smelling.

William Shakespeare
English playwright

When you were a tadpole and I was a fish, in the Paleozoic time, and side by side on the ebbing tide, we sprawled through the ooze and slime... My heart was rife with the joy of life, for I loved you even then.

Langdon Smith
Writer

Make love now, by night and by day, in winter and in summer... You are in the world for that and the rest of life is nothing but vanity, illusion, waste. There is only one science, love; only one riches, love; only one policy, love. To make love is all the law, and the prophets.

Anatole France
French writer

Ah, love, let us be true to one another! for the world, which seems to lie before us like a land of dreams, so various, so beautiful, so new, hath really neither joy, nor love, nor light, nor certitude, nor peace, nor help for pain; and we are here as on a darkling plain swept with confused alarms of struggle and flight, where ignorant armies clash by night.

Matthew Arnold
British poet

If there hadn't been women we'd still be squatting in a cave eating raw meat, because we made civilization in order to impress our girl friends. And they tolerated it and let us go ahead and play with our toys.

Orson Welles
American filmmaker

The eyes those silent tongues of love.

Miguel de Cervantes
Spanish writer

Then women enter whose lips and dazzling teeth seduce the eye; but meek and virtuous, trained in every art; fit sharers of play-time, so soft their flesh and delicate their bones. O Soul come back and let them ease your woe!

Ch' Ü Yüan
Chinese poet

The sexual instincts are the most malleable of any instincts. Let them be repressed, let their direct aim be denied them, and they will soon assume unrecognizable forms, from the depth of vice to the highest exaltation of art and religion.

Robert Briffault
British surgeon

If you live in rock and roll, as I do, you see the reality of sex, of male lust and women being aroused by male lust. It attracts women. It doesn't repel them.

Camille Paglia
American educator

The eternal female draws us onward.

Johann Wolfgang von Goethe
German poet

The pleasure of the act of love is gross and brief and brings loathing after it.

Petronius (called Arbiter)
Roman writer

There is love of course. And then there's life, its enemy.

Jean Anouilh
French playwright

Never miss a chance to have sex or appear on television.

Gore Vidal
American novelist

Every love is the love before in a duller dress.

Dorothy Parker
American humorist

Why are women…so much more interesting to men than men are
to women?

Virginia Woolf
English novelist

Lust after Women and Marriage Too

Men do lust after women, more than the reverse, primarily because
wooing and winning women are the paths toward reproduction. Women,
with more at stake in child birth and care, are more objective in choos-
ing mates, so it seems, concerned more as they are in quality offspring.
It's been said that women want relationships that will help their reproductive goals. For that they trade sex. Men want sex. For that they trade
relationships, somewhat reluctantly.

The substance of our lives is women. All other things are irrel-
evancies, hypocrisies, subterfuges. We sit talking of sports and
politics, and all the while our hearts are filled with memories of
women and the capture of women.

George Moore
Irish novelist

[He manifested] all Sappho's famous signs—his voice faltered, his
face flushed up, his eyes glanced steathily, a sudden sweat broke
out on his skin, the beatings of his heart were irregular and violent.

Plutarch
Roman historian

He fell from his horse as mighty as a mountain, like a leaf that the
wind rips from the tree. The brain in his head had begun to boil
from the fire in his heart; heart had fled from body and sense from
head… The rosy cheeks had turned the colour of saffron; his wine-
coloured lips blue as the sky. The hue of life had deserted his face,
the insignia of love appeared there in its stead.

Fakhr-ud-din Gurani
Persian poet

Marriage is the only adventure open to the cowardly.

Voltaire
French writer

Love hath made thee a tame snake.

William Shakespeare
English playwright

He that hath wife and children hath given hostages to fortune; for they are impediments to great enterprises, either of virtue or mischief.

Francis Bacon
English philosopher

The fundamental trouble with marriage is that it shakes a man's confidence in himself, and so greatly diminishes his general competence and effectiveness. His habit of mind becomes that of a commander who has lost a decisive and calamitous battle. He never quite trusts himself thereafter.

H. L. Mencken
American critic

Win her with gifts, if she respect not words.

William Shakespeare
English playwright

The majority of persons choose their wives with as little prudence as they eat. They see a trull with nothing else to recommend her but a pair of thighs and choice hunkers, and so smart to void their seed that they marry her at once. They imagine they can live in marvelous contentment with handsome feet and ambrosial buttocks. Most men are accredited fools shortly after they leave the womb.

Edward Dahlberg
American author

Woman is the dominant sex. Men have to do all sorts of stuff to prove that they are worthy of women's attention.

Camille Paglia
American educator

Words are women, deeds are men.

George Herbert
English metaphysical poet

It is a wise father that knows his own child.

William Shakespeare
English playwright

My mother saith he is my father. Yet for myself I know it not. For no man knoweth who hath begotten him.

Homer
Greek poet

I know of nothing so ludicrous as to see a father talking about his children. "My wife's children," he should say. Did you never feel the falseness of your position, had you never any pinpricks of doubt.

August Strindberg
Swedish writer

The family is based on the supremacy of the men, the express purpose being to produce children of undisputed paternity. Such paternity is demanded because these children are later to come into their father's property as his natural heirs.

Friedrich Engels
German socialist

The cuckoo then in every tree; mocks married men; for thus sings he, "Cuckoo, cuckoo, cuckoo; O word of fear; unpleasing to a married ear.

William Shakespeare
English playwright

"Supposing that we should have a third one?" Here said Ado Annie, "the girl who can't say no." "Had better look a lot like me!" said her fiancee.

Oklahoma
Stage play

It is a truth universally acknowledged, that a single man in possession of good fortune, must be in want of a wife.

Jane Austen
English novelist

The desire of a man for a woman is not directed at her because she is a human being, but because she is a woman. That she is a human being is of no concern to him.

Immanuel Kant
German philosopher

Love has been in perpetual strife with monogamy.

Ellen Key
Swedish feminist

Maybe today's successful marriage is when a man is in love with his wife and only one other woman.

Matt Basile
American private detective

The Western custom of one wife and hardly any mistresses.

Saki (Hector Hugh Munro)
British writer

What men desire is a virgin who is a whore.

Edward Dahlberg
American author

If women didn't exist, all the money in the world would have no meaning.

Aristotle Onassis
Greek businessman

Without women, the beginning of our life would be helpless; the middle devoid of pleasure; and the end of consolation.

Victor Joseph Etienne de Jouy
French writer

Young men want to be faithful, and are not; old men want to be faithless, and cannot: that is all one can say.

Oscar Wilde
Irish playwright

Tumescence is the period between pubescence and senescence.

Robert Byrne
English poet

You may build castles in the air, and fume, and fret, and grow thin and lean, and pale and ugly, if you please, but I tell you, no man worth having is true to his wife, or can be true to his wife, or ever was, or will be so.

Sir John Vanbrugh
British playwright

The natural man has only two primal passions, to get and to beget.

Sir William Osler
Canadian scientist

I'd like to have a girl, and I'm saving my money so I can get a good one.

Bob Nickman
Writer

The Nature of Women

For centuries women have been known to be a major force in determining the structure of civilization, primarily because of their drive to reproduce, and because of their gaze on quality men. Clearly, women have driven the engine of social interactions. Cognizant of their changing needs they quickly switch strategies, leaving men wondering.

In the theory of gender I began from zero. There is no masculine power or privilege I did not covet. But slowly, step by step, decade by decade, I was forced to acknowledge that even a woman of abnormal will cannot escape her hormonal identity.

Camille Paglia
American educator

The contemporary woman's liberation drive toward a decrease in sexual differentiation, to the extent that it is leading toward androgyny and unisexual values, implies a social and cultural death-wish and the end of the civilization that endorses it. The scientific and historical records show that all the way from unicellular organisms to human beings, progress in evolution has been stimulated by an increase in *sexual differentiation*.

Amaury de Riencourt
Sex historian

Wondrous hole! Magical hole! Dazzling influential hole! Noble and effulgent hole! From this hole everything follows logically: first the baby, then the placenta, then, for years and years and years until death, a way of life. It is all logic, and she who lives by the hole will live also by its logic. It is, appropriately, logic with a hole in it.

Cynthia Ozick
American novelist

A young nun am I, sixteen years of age; shaven in my young maidenhood... I'll leave the drums, I'll leave the bells, and the chants and the yells, and all the interminable, exasperating, religious chatter! I'll go downhill, and find me a young and handsome lover—let him scold me, beat me! Kick or ill-treat me! I will *not* become a Buddha! I will not mumble mita, prajna, para!

Lin Yutang
Chinese writer

I use to be a virgin, but I gave it up because there was no money in it.

Marsha Warfield
Writer

I only have two rules for my newly born daughter: she will dress well and never have sex.

John Malkovich
American stage and screen actor

It would be futile to attempt to fit women into a masculine pattern of attitudes, skills and abilities and disastrous to force them to suppress their specifically female characteristics and abilities by keeping up the pretense that there are no differences between the sexes.

Arianna Stassinopoulos
Greek author

Women are natural guerrillas. Scheming, we nestle into the enemy's bed, avoiding open warfare, watching the options, playing the odds.

Sally Kempton
American author

Women run to extremes; they are either better or worse than men.

Jean de La Bruyère
French satirist

Woman's at best a contradiction still.

Alexander Pope
British poet

I don't think a prostitute is more moral than a wife, but they are doing the same thing.

Prince Philip
Duke of Edinburgh

When lowering clouds shut in the day, when streets are mired with sticky clay, when husband lingers far away, the flirt becomes supremely gay.

The Panchatantra
Translated by Arthur W. Ryder

One's prime is elusive. You little girls, when you grow up, must be on the alert to recognize your prime at whatever time of your life it may occur. You must then live it to the full.

Muriel Spark
British novelist

A man is as old as his feeling, a woman as old as she looks.

Mortimer Collins
British writer

From birth to age 18, a girl needs good parents, from 18 to 35 she needs good looks, from 35–55 she needs a good personality, and from 55 on she needs cash.

Sophie Tucker
American humorist

Ah, wasteful woman, she who may on her sweet self set her own price, knowing he cannot choose but pay, how has she cheapen'd paradise.

Coventry Patmore
British poet

If civilization had been left in female hands we would still be living in grass huts.

Camille Paglia
American educator

A man in the house is worth two in the street.

Mae West
American humorist

It is better to have a prosaic husband and to take a romantic lover.

Stendhal
French author

This man, she reasons, as she looks at her husband, is a poor fish. But he is the nearest I can get to the big one that got away.

Nigel Dennis
British writer

No woman marries for money; they are all clever enough, before marrying a millionaire to fall in love with him first.

Cesare Pavese
Italian novelist

A woman talks to one man, looks at a second, and thinks of a third.

Bhartrihari
Indian grammarian

Trust your husband, adore your husband, and get as much as you can in your own name.

Mother's advice to Joan Rivers
American comedian

As I walk along the Bois Bou-long, with an independent air, you can hear the girls declare, 'He must be a millionaire,' You can hear them sigh and wish to die, you see them wink the other eye at the man who broke the bank at Monte Carlo.

Fred Gilbert
British songwriter

Women exist in the main solely for the propagation of the species.

Arthur Schopenhauer
German philosopher

For the woman, the man is a means: the end is always the child.

Friedrich Nietzsche
German philosopher

There's only one pretty child in the world, and every mother has it.

Proverb

Oh my son's my son till he gets him a wife, but my daughter's my daughter all her life.

Dinah Mulock Craik
British writer

Woman is always fickle and changing.

Virgil
Roman poet

O tiger's heart wrapp'd in a woman's hide!

William Shakespeare
English playwright

Marriage, Reproduction, and Children

Philosophers, historians, and others have long sensed the social and biological significance of the family. They understood the thread of life linking generations and the rough corners surrounding successful reproduction.

As is the generations of leaves, so is that of humanity. The wind scatters the leaves on the ground, but the live timber burgeons with leaves again in the season of spring returning. So one generation of men will grow while another dies.

Homer
Greek poet

'Tis a happy thing to be the father unto many sons.

William Shakespeare
English playwright

One does not marry for oneself, whatever may be said; a man marries as much, or more, for his posterity, for his family; the usage and interest of marriage touch our race beyond ourselves. Thus it is a kind of incest to employ, in this venerable and sacred parentage, the efforts and the extravagance of amorous license.

Michel de Montaigne
French philosopher

Great with child; and longing...for stewed prunes.

William Shakespeare
English playwright

The cocks may crow, but it's the hen that lays the egg.

Margaret Thatcher
British Prime Minister

Living substance conquers the frenzy of destruction only in the ecstasy of procreation.

Walter Benjamin
German philosopher

Happy marriages are well known to be rare; just because it lies in the nature of marriage that its chief end is not the present but the coming generation.

Arthur Schopenhauer
German philosopher

Literature is mostly about having sex and not much about having children. Life is the other way around.

David Lodge
British author

I learned that...love is only a dirty trick played on us to achieve the continuation of the species.

W. Somerset Maugham
English novelist

Mothers are fonder than fathers of their children because they are more certain they are their own.

Aristotle
Greek philosopher

In its essence, the delight of sexual love, the genetic spasm, is a sensation of resurrection, of renewing our life in another, for only in others can we renew our life and so perpetuate ourselves.

Miguel de Unamuno
Spanish writer

Motherhood is neither a duty nor a privilege, but simply the way that humanity can satisfy the desire for physical immortality and triumph over the fear of death.

Rebecca West
British writer

Blessed indeed is the man who hears many gentle voices call him father.

Lydia M. Child
American abolitionist

Every new baby is a blind desperate vote for survival: people who find themselves unable to register an effective political protest against extermination do so by a biological act.

Lewis Mumford
American social philosopher

The value of marriage is not that adults produce children but that children produce adults.

Peter de Vries
American writer

One can love a child, perhaps, more deeply than one can love another adult, but it is rash to assume that the child feels any love in return.

George Orwell
British writer

How sharper than a serpent's tooth it is to have a thankless child.

William Shakespeare
English playwright

What is an adult? A child blown up by age.

Simone de Beauvoir
French novelist

In the duel of sex, woman fights from a dreadnought and man from an open raft.

H. L. Mencken
American critic

Those marriages generally abound most with love and constancy that are preceded by a long courtship.

Joseph Addison
English essayist

The relation of the sexes...is really the invisible central point of all action and conduct... It is the cause of war and the end of peace; the basis of what is serious, and the aim of the jest; the inexhaustible source of wit, the key to all illusions, and the meaning of all mysterious hints.

Arthur Schopenhauer
German philosopher

It is a woman's business to get married as soon as possible, and a man's to keep unmarried as long as he can.

George Bernard Shaw
British playwright

Sex drive: A physical craving that begins in adolescence and ends at marriage.

Robert Byrne
Scottish poet

Hanging and wiving goes by destiny.

William Shakespeare
English playwright

By the time you swear you're his, shivering and sighing, and he vows his passion is infinite, undying—one of you is lying.

Dorothy Parker
American humorist

Oh what lies there are in kisses.

Heinrich Heine
German poet

When two people decide to get a divorce, it isn't a sign that they "don't understand" one another, but a sign that they have, at last, begun.

Helen Rowland
American journalist

Mi advise tu them who are about tu begin, in arnest, the jurney ov live, is to take their harte in one hand and a club in the other.

Josh Billings
American humorist

Love is a kind of warfare.

Ovid
Roman poet

Every woman should marry—and no man.

Benjamin Disraeli
British statesman

...for no man can know who was his father. No trust is to be placed in women.

Homer
Greek poet

The Seven-Year Itch.

George Axelrod
American screenwriter

Physically, a man is a man for a much longer time than a woman is a woman.

Honoré de Balzac
French writer

I doubt whether any girl would be satisfied with her lover's mind if she knew the whole of it.

Anthony Trollope
British novelist

Fornication is a lapse from one marriage into another.

Clement of Alexandria
Church Father

The lower one's vitality, the more sensitive one is to great art.

William Shakespeare
English playwright

The man's desire is for the woman; but the woman's desire is rarely other than for the desire of the man.

Samuel Taylor Coleridge
English poet

The dread of loneliness is greater than the fear of bondage, so we get married.

Cyril Connolly
English essayist

A young man loves women; a middle-aged man loves struggle; and an old man loves money.

Confucius
Chinese philosopher

Green-eyed Jealousy

Our selfish genes reach out for domination in all areas of endeavor. In our mating it's the same, with both men and women seeking advantages. Men have a special problem, not shared by women; men are ultimately unsure of their paternity. As a result men tend to be jealous of their women, fearing infidelity and cuckoldry. Jealousy rages like a fire in the hearts of men. Women are less concerned with their men's fidelity, but they are jealous of male partners who bestow resources on other women. The differences in the form of jealousies follow the differences in reproductive strategies.

The hood-winked husband shows his anger, and the word jealous is flung in his face. Jealous husband equals betrayed husband. And there are women who look upon jealousy as synonymous with impotence, so that the betrayed husband can only shut his eyes, powerless in the face of such accusations.

August Strindberg
Swedish dramatist

O curse of marriage, that we can call these delicate creatures ours, and not their appetites! I had rather be a toad and live upon the vapor of a dungeon than keep a corner in the thing I love for others' uses.

William Shakespeare
English playwright

O, beware, my lord, of jealousy; it is the green-ey'd monster which doth mock the meat it feeds on.

William Shakespeare
English playwright

No lover, if he be of good faith, and sincere, will deny he would prefer to see his mistress dead than unfaithful.

Marquis de Sade
French author

Those who are faithful know only the trivial side of love; it is the faithless who know love's tragedies.

Oscar Wilde
Irish playwright

Jealousy contains more of self-love than of love.

Francois, Duc de la Rochefoucauld
French writer

He married a woman to stop her getting away. Now she's there all day.

Philip Larkin
British poet

Jealousy is one of those affective states, like grief, that may be ascribed as normal...

Sigmund Freud
Austrian psychoanalyst

Beauty, Health and Commitment

Women use beauty as a spear to penetrate the hearts of men. And well they can, as beauty reflects health and reproductive potential— all that males desire. Thus, females parade their beauty before males, always seeking attention of quality males. Males simply lust after beauty.

Nature has given hearts to bulls, hoofs to horses, swiftness to hares, the power of swimming to fishes, of flying to birds, understand-ing to men. She has nothing more for women save beauty. Beauty is proof against spears and shields. She who is beautiful is more formidable than fire and iron.

Anacreon
Greek lyric poet

Beauty provoketh thieves sooner than gold.

William Shakespeare
English playwright

No, we have been as usual asking the wrong question. It does not matter a hoot what the mockingbird on the chimney is singing... The real and proper question is: Why is it beautiful?

Annie Dillard
American poet

Thou art a friend, a woman's shape doth shield thee.

William Shakespeare
English playwright

Beauty itself doth of itself persuade the eyes of men without an orator.

William Shakespeare
English playwright

Health is beauty, and the most perfect health is the most perfect beauty.

William Shenstone
British poet

EGGHEAD WED HOURGLASS. On marriage of playwright Arthur Miller to Marilyn Monroe.

Anonymous
Variety *headline*

Sex and beauty are inseparable, like life and consciousness.

D. H. Lawrence
English novelist

Beauty is eternity gazing at itself in a mirror.

Kahlil Gibran
Lebanese poet

A poor beauty finds more lovers than husbands.

British proverb

Beauty is only the promise of happiness.

Stendhal
French author

Exuberance is beauty.

William Blake
English poet

I know not how to conceive the good, apart from the pleasures of taste, sexual pleasure, the pleasures of sound, and the pleasures of beautiful forms.

Diogenes Laërtius
Greek philosopher

It has been said that a pretty face is a passport. But it's not, it's a visa, and it runs out fast.

Julie Burchill
British journalist

Whether a pretty woman grants or withholds her favors, she always likes to be asked for them.

Ovid
Roman poet

It is the common wonder of all men, how among so many millions of faces, there should be more alike.

Thomas Brown
British physician

There is no excellent beauty that hath not some strangeness in the proportion.

Francis Bacon
English philosopher

You must go to bed with friends or whores, where money makes up the difference in beauty or desire.

W. H. Auden
English poet

Remember that the most beautiful things in the world are the most useless, peacocks and lilies for instance.

John Ruskin
British art critic

It is better to be the first with an ugly woman than the hundredth with a beauty.

Pearl Buck
American novelist

The Lord prefers common-looking people. That is why he makes so many of them.

Abraham Lincoln
American president

We tolerate shapes in human beings that would horrify us if we saw them in a horse.

W. R. Inge
British churchman

Assortative Mating

If you find someone like yourself, you find some of your own genes. Therefore, helping someone who shares your genes is like helping your own genes. Assortment for similar traits tends to stabilize relationships and make reproduction possible. Historians knew little of this, but they did realize that couples did assort on the basis of similar traits.

Tell me what company thou keepest, and I'll tell thee what thou art.

Miguel de Cervantes
Spanish writer

Well, I said, the principle has been already laid down that the best of either sex should be united with the best as often, and the inferior with the inferior, as seldom as possible; and that they should rear the offspring of the other sort of union, but not of the other, if the flock is to be maintained in first-rate condition. Now these goings on must be a secret which the rulers know, or there will be further danger of our herd, as the Guardians may be termed breaking out in rebellion.

Plato
Greek philosopher

The Master said… "Have no friends not equal to yourself."

Confucius
Chinese philosopher

Who ever loved, that loved not a first sight?

Louis XIV
French king

Every man is like the company he is wont to keep.

Euripides
Greek dramatist

Friends have all things in common.

Plato
Greek philosopher

What is a friend? A single soul dwelling in two bodies.

Aristotle
Greek philosopher

A friend is, as it were, a second self.

Marcus Tullius Cicero
Roman statesman

We go together, Laurie, I don't know why. Maybe like guns and ammunition go together.

John Dall to Peggy Cummins
Movie: Gun Crazy

The thing that's between us is fascination, and the fascination resides in our being alike. Whether you're a man or woman, the fascination resides in finding out that we're alike.

Marguerite Duras
French author

There is a lady sweet and kind, was never face so pleased my mind; I did but see her passing by, and yet I love her 'til I die.

Anonymous

Those who practice the same profession recognize each other instinctively; likewise those who practice the same vice.

Marcel Proust
French novelist

When novelists and poets write about irrational love, we often know it's true. Men seem more driven than women, often making romantic and marital decisions based upon sexual lust. Women do that less frequently, striving more for material and non-material benefits. Women are ultimately concerned with children; men are concerned with sex and paternity. Women cannot be fooled about their motherhood, but men live with the constant anxiety of uncertainty, hence their jealousy and reduced commitment to parental responsibilities.

Love, marriage, and children—the big three of evolution—are known for what they are by philosophers and playwrights, disguised as irresistible beauty. We look beneath the beauty and strive for genetic similarity in our relations—love at first sight, so it is said—helping us to bond tightly and reproduce our own kind. Kings and sages, without benefit of genetic theory, long ago told us it was so.

3

The Dark Side of Human Nature

The Criminal Within

The sociological view of crime is that criminals are made, not born. Poverty, lack of education, broken families, and unemployment are some of the major factors blamed (Reiss & Roth, 1993). Social and demographic factors do affect the expression of crime, but the potential appears rooted in evolution. Crime is a human behavior aimed at acquisition of resources, extension of kin or group influence, protection from exploitation, or revenge for wrongdoing (Wilson & Hernstein, 1985). For some, it is also a sport that gives pleasure (Hare, 1993).

The incidence of crime is affected by the environment, just as any other complex survival response. I (Thiessen, 1996) have expressed this gene-environment interaction in this way: "Evolutionary strategies for social competition, cost/benefit analyses, resource acquisition, and mate choice can also bias individuals toward murder, mayhem and madness. *Homo sapiens* never evolved adaptive strategies for criminal behavior *de nova*, only strategies for the preservation and propagation of selfish genes. Thus, there are no genetic and evolutionary *determinants* for criminal acts, only genetic and adaptive *inclinations* for survival and reproduction, sometimes expressed in extreme ways. Given these, along with a permissive environment and individual differences in susceptibility, the likelihood of anti-social acts is substantial." From the evolutionary perspective, criminal behavior is potential in us all, but is only realized under environmental conditions that bring it out.

Criminality tends to run in families, independent of general environmental effects, showing that genes do sometimes bias individuals toward criminal acts (Allen, Beck, with the Bureau of Justice Statistics). For example, studies by geneticists DiLalla and Gottesman (1991) of identical and non-identical twins conclude that about a third of the variations in adolescent delinquent behavior is genetic. Mednick and his colleagues (1984) additionally show that adopted offspring follow the criminal behavioral pattern of the biological fathers, not their adopting fathers. Thus, the chances of a male becoming a criminal is significantly increased if his biological father had been convicted of a crime, regardless of the family social environment. Again, it should be emphasized that it is not "criminal genes" that are the cause of crime, but genetic differences among individuals in the susceptibility to environments that evoke such behaviors. A restraining environment will reduce the expression of these genes; a permissive environment will increase their expression. A good distinction to keep in mind is that crime is made up of two parts, the number of criminals in the population and the number of crimes per criminal. The first is called prevalence, and is essentially a measure of the genetic predisposition for crime; the second is the incidence of crime, a measure of the actual frequency with which criminals commit unlawful behaviors. It is the incidence of crime that is modifiable by the environment.

Gene variations among individuals act to change the frequency of criminality by acting through complex neural and physiological processes. For example, criminal behavior has been linked to psychopathy, hyperactivity, low intelligence, certain morphological traits, brain trauma, hormonal variations, brain neurotransmitters, and specific gene mutations that affect metabolic processes (Brunner, Nelsen, van Zandvoort, Abeling, van Gennip, Wolters, Kulper, Ropers & van Oost, 1993; Dabbs & Morris, 1990; Hernstein & Murray, 1994; Reiss & Roth, 1993; Thiessen, 1996; Wilson & Hernstein, 1985). Several of these studies suggest that genetically influenced traits can predispose individuals toward criminal behavior.

Variations at a number of levels may elevate the incidence of criminal acts, but it is also true that many individuals are not affected by similar traits. There is obviously a complex interaction between the consequences of natural selection for adaptive traits, individual differences in genetic and physiologic attributes, and the nature of the environment. While we don't have definitive answers at this point, there is considerable promise that the complexity of criminal behavior will be parsed into its individual components.

Family Violence

Murder and abuse of sexual partners and children have recently been interpreted in evolutionary terms (Daly & Wilson, 1988). Worldwide, males are more likely to murder females than the reverse. Moreover, they typically aim their fury at partners when their paternity is in question. Presumably, males have evolved a more physically aggressive nature. Beyond that, however, if there is a question of the female's fidelity in a relationship, the male is more inclined to abandon the partnership, and in some cases even murder the mother and the offspring. He would rather jettison the investment if he is not sure that the genes he is caring for are his own, or if he believes that the female might be sexually open to other males.

The female has evolved somewhat different strategies, as she was not evolved to aggressively compete for matings AND she always knows that her child is hers—no concern there. Still, she will also abandon her reproductive investment if it appears that she cannot care for the offspring, or if she judges that an offspring later is better than an offspring now. She may also abuse or murder her male partner if he does not contribute to her reproductive success (Straus & Gelles, 1990).

Social interactions are conflictual by nature, as individuals and sexes differ in their biological designs and their reproductive strategies. In general, if the cost of parental care is too high, the reproductive efforts may be terminated or abandoned. Child neglect and abuse are decreased to the degree that the parents share genes in common with their children (Daly & Wilson, 1981).

It may be helpful to pause here to emphasize that social strategies are often implemented unconsciously—typically we are not aware of why we react toward others as we do. The fears we feel, the elation we experience, and the deceptions we employ are products of natural selection, not reactions to conscious thought. They may seem irrational, and they may no longer be adaptive in our highly complex and changing culture, but they may still make sense in terms of our earlier evolutionary history.

The statistics and biological implications surrounding crime are grim and unsettling, but there is little new under the sun. Biologists pursue the problem, looking for deep and coherent explanations, but we have always known what we are, like it or not.

The Darkness Within

The Depth of Criminality

The most outstanding trait of man is his tendency toward criminality, aggression, and self-aggrandizement—the full expression of the selfish gene. Throughout history many have suspected that criminality went deep into our personality. Perhaps because of its universality and its persistence in all environments, crime has seemed to be a predictable mode of human behavior.

> All, all is theft, all is unceasing and rigorous competition in nature; the desire to make off with the substance of others is the foremost—the most legitimate—passion nature has bred into us... and, without doubt, the most agreeable one.
>
> *Marquis de Sade*
> *French author*

> If only there were evil people somewhere insidiously committing evil deeds and it were necessary only to separate them from the rest of us and destroy them. But the line dividing good and evil cuts through the heart of every human being. And who is willing to destroy a piece of his own heart?
>
> *Aleksandr Solzhenitsyn*
> *Russian writer*

> Nature allows all, by its murderous laws; incest and rape, all theft and parricide, all Sodom's pleasures. Sappho's lesbian games, all that destroys and send men to their graves.
>
> *Marquis de Sade*
> *French author*

> Wolves which fatten upon lambs, lambs consumed by wolves, the strong who immolate the weak, the weak victims of the strong: there you have Nature, there you have her intentions, there you have her scheme: a perpetual action and reaction, a host of vices, a host of virtues, in one word, a perfect equilibrium resulting from the equality of good and evil on earth.
>
> *Marquis de Sade*
> *French author*

> For centuries the death penalty, often accompanied by barbarous refinements, has been trying to hold crime in check: yet crime persists. Why? Because the instincts that are warring in man are not, as the law claims, constant forces in a state of equilibrium.
>
> *Albert Camus*
> *French writer*

Murder, like talent, seems occasionally to run in families.

G. H. Lewes
British philosopher

Happy the hare at morning, for she cannot read the hunter's waking thoughts.

W. H. Auden
English poet

No, it is not only our fate but our business to lose innocence, and once we have lost that, it is futile to attempt to picnic in Eden.

Elizabeth Bowen
Irish novelist

No arts; no letters; no society; and which is worst of all, continual fear, and danger of violent death; and the life of man, solitary, nasty, brutish, and short.

Thomas Hobbes
British philosopher

After all, crime is only a left-handed form of human endeavor.

John Huston
American filmmaker

It is a power stronger than will...could a stone escape from the laws of gravity? Impossible, impossible, for evil to form an alliance with good.

Isidore Ducasse, Comte de Lautréamont
French poet

Nothing is evil which is according to nature.

Marcus Aurelius Antonius
Roman emperor

Murder...like all destruction, is one of the first laws of nature.

Marquis de Sade
French writer

A man who lives with nature is used to violence and is companionable with death. There is more violence in an English hedgerow than in the meanest streets of a great city.

P. D. James
British mystery writer

If you prick us do we not bleed? If you tickle us do we not laugh?
If you poison us do we not die? And if you wrong us shall we not
revenge?

William Shakespeare
English playwright

This is the law of the Yukon, that only the strong shall thrive; that
surely the weak shall perish and only the Fit survive.

Robert William Service
Canadian poet

Natural selection, as it has operated in human history, favors not
only the clever but the murderous.

Barbara Ehrenreich
American author

The Paradox of Living

Good and evil inhabit the same hearts of men and women, moving
with unpredictable consequences.

What a chimera, then, is man! What a novelty, what a monster,
what a chaos, what a contradiction, what a prodigy! Judge of all
things, helpless earthworm, depository of truth, a sink of uncertainty and error. Glory and scum of the universe.

Blaise Pascal
French philosopher

Man is physically as well as metaphysically a thing of shreds and
patches, borrowed unequally from good and bad ancestors, and a
misfit from the start.

Ralph Waldo Emerson
American poet

We should expect the best and the worst from mankind, as from
the weather.

Marquis de Luc de Chapiers Vauvenargues
French novelist

Man has much more to fear from the passions of his fellow creatures than from the convulsions of the elements.

Edward Gibbon
British writer

There is so much good in the worst of us, and so much bad in the best of us, that it hardly becomes any of us to talk about the rest of us.

Anonymous

There is nothing either good or bad but thinking makes it so.

William Shakespeare
English playwright

The web of our life is of a mingled yarn, good and ill together.

William Shakespeare
English playwright

There is an odd illusion—it is called good and evil.

Friedrich Nietzsche
German philosopher

Nature, in her indifference, makes no distinction between good and evil.

Anatole France
French writer

Recognizing the Beast Within

Ever since recorded history we have recognized that evil is within us, not forced on us by those around us. The selfish gene is ours. Look deeply within yourself.

The study of crime begins with the knowledge of oneself. All that you despise, all that you loathe, all that you reject, all that you condemn and seek to convert by punishment springs from you.

Henry Miller
American author

It is silly to go on pretending that under the skin we are all brothers. The truth is more likely that we are all cannibals, assassins, traitors, liars, hypocrites, poltroons.

Henry Miller
American author

Every man is a potential murderer.

Clarence S. Darrow
American lawyer

If a murder, anybody might have done it. Burglary or pocket-picking wanted 'prenticeship. Not so murder. We were all of us up to that.

Charles Dickens
English author

Uncontrolled violence is a fault of youth.

Lucius Annaeus Seneca
Roman philosopher

The belief in a supernatural source of evil is not necessary; men alone are quite capable of every wickedness.

Joseph Conrad
English novelist

The only vice that I perceive in the universe is Avarice; all the others, whatever name they be known by, are only variations, degrees of this one.

Morelly
French utopian

Every man has a beast within him.

Frederick the Great
Prussian king

It takes two to make a murder. There are born victims, born to have their throats cut.

Aldous Huxley
British novelist

For nothing can seem foul to those that win.

> *William Shakespeare*
> *English playwright*

Where we are, there's daggers in men's smiles: the near in blood, the nearer bloody.

> *William Shakespeare*
> *English playwright*

We are all murderers and prostitutes—no matter to what culture, society, class, nation one belongs, no matter how normal, moral or mature, one takes oneself to be.

> *R. D. Laing*
> *British psychiatrist*

All men naturally hate each other.

> *Blaise Pascal*
> *French philosopher*

If poverty is the mother of crime, stupidity is its father.

> *Jean de La Bruyère*
> *French satirist*

A generous and noble spirit cannot be expected to dwell in the breasts of men who are struggling for their daily bread.

> *Dionysius of Halicarnassus*
> *Greek historian*

The Thin Edge Between Love and Murder

Ah, yes, love and murder, murder and love—two forces stuck together by the uncertainties of male and female bonds. Jealousy and greed are seen between the lines, illustrating the biological reasons for love and murder.

Murder is born of love, and love attains the greatest intensity in murder.

> *Octave Mirbeau*
> *French journalist*

When we want to read of the deeds that are done for love, whither do we turn? To the murder column.

George Bernard Shaw
British playwright

Elyot: It doesn't suit women to be promiscuous. Amanda: It doesn't suit men for women to be promiscuous.

Noël Coward
British playwright

Of all the emotions, there is none more violent than love.

Marcus Tullius Cicero
Roman statesman

No more deadly curse has ever been given by Nature to man than carnal pleasure. There is no criminal purpose and no evil deed which the lust for pleasure will not drive man to undertake.

Archytas of Tarentum
Pythagorean mathematician and philosopher

A lot of different guys are considered very sensible until they get tangled up with a doll, and maybe loving her, and the first thing anybody knows they hop out of windows, or shoot themselves, or shoot somebody else, and I can see where even a guy like Dave the Dude may go daffy over a doll.

Damon Runyon
American journalist

There is a woman in every case; as soon as they bring me a report, I say, "Look for the woman."

Alexandre Dumas
French playwright

See how love and murder will out.

William Congreve
British dramatist

Man is the hunter; woman is his game: the sleek and shining creatures of the chase, we hunt them for the beauty of their skins.

Alfred Lord Tennyson
English poet

Lust's passion will be served; it demands, it militates, it tyrannizes.

Marquis de Sade
French author

The Sweet Smell of Crime

Most biological drives are shaded with desirable emotions, coupling such things as sex and love, escape and relief, victory and euphoria. All drives have their hedonistic correlates. It has to be, or the drives wouldn't function. For example, sex would never occur unless it felt good. Nature makes the connection.

Little wonder, then, that crime makes us feel good, at least when successful. It can also make us feel guilty, but the question is who has not felt the thrill of a small theft, a slight advantage, or a large successful lie. Crime can absorb us—a shocking reality of life. I came to the conclusion many years ago that almost all crime is due to the repressed desire for aesthetic expression.

Evelyn Waugh
British novelist

Evil has repute and power; good is passive, anonymous.

A. J. Dunning
Cardiologist

For a good cause crime is virtuous.

Publius Syrus
Syrian-born Latin writer

Hatred can at times be a positively joyous emotion.

Simone De Beauvoir
French writer

Revenge, at first though sweet, bitter ere long back on itself recoils.

John Milton
English poet

There is a heroism in crime as well as in virtue. Vice and infamy have their altars and their religion.

William Hazlitt
British essayist

In violence, we forget who we are.

Mary McCarthy
American writer

My near'st and dearest enemy.

William Shakespeare
English playwright

The Marquis de Sade and many others have told us that crime is a part of our nature, existing uncomfortably side by side with love and sacrifice. The evil lies within, bubbling forth in jealousy, hate, and revenge. It is our evolutionary core, known for all of history, part of our adaptive nature, wrapped in pleasure. "How do I love (hate) you; let me count the ways." The worst possibility, one that could keep one awake, is that evil is not evil at all, but simply one more indifferent adaptation provided us through eons of natural selection.

4

The Duality of the Human Brain

Does not our brain carry the promise of independence from biology? Have we not stepped beyond our basic nature? Are we not capable of delivering ourselves from evil?

The answers seem obvious. It was our mushrooming brain, acquired during evolution for adaptive traits, that gave us power over our environment and our adversaries. It was that same brain that allowed us to move out of Africa and spread into every crevice of the world. And it was our brain that gave us language, art, science, and politics. Clearly, our complex brain provided the roots of our achievements—the nucleus of our destiny. But, has it set us free?

Today we are beginning to understand the evolution, structure, and function of brain complexity. On the average the human brain increased in size during the last 2.5 million years by one-millionth of a percent per generation (Calvin, 1990). That may not sound like much, but added up, the change was from about 450 cubic centimeters to nearly three times that. Paleobiologist Elisabeth Vrba (1985) believes that major climate shifts were associated with hominid speciations and brain increases, leading to the rise of *Homo sapiens*. The process began between 5 and 6 million years ago as global cooling eliminated subtropical rain forests. As a result the ancestors of man were forced to adapt to the increasing importance of savannah grasslands. This major change was followed by shorter cycles of alternating warming and cooling. Australopithecine species appeared, setting off the chain of speciations leading to *Homo habilis*, *Homo erectus*, *Neanderthal*, and *Homo sapiens* (Johanson & Johanson, 1994; Leaky & Lewin, 1992). The correlations between climate changes and evolution are rough, but do suggest that they drove brain complexity (Vrba, 1985).

We know more about the structure and function of the human brain than we know about its origins. First, there has been a disproportionate expansion of brain size relative to body size in primates, especially for

Homo sapiens and our immediate ancestors (Eccles, 1989; Jerrison, 1985). The cortex, or mantle of the brain became more complex, shifting several primitive functions to new and more complex regions.

The second thing we know is that the brain is regionally specified according to functions; that is, different regions of the brain control different physiological and behavioral functions (Crick, 1994). Older, more primitive functions, are relegated to an evolutionary older area, called the limbic system. Neurophysiologist Paul MacLean (1970) provided the evolutionary metaphor when he spoke of the "triune" nature of the brain, suggesting that the mammalian brain retains the anatomical and chemical features of our reptilian and early mammalian ancestors. These are the vertebrate brain regions responsible for some of our most primitive behaviors of sex, aggression, feeding, and thermoregulation. To some extent, then, the evolution of the human brain was based on early vertebrate structures and functions, leading, finally, to the newer mammalian components responsible for abstract thought, consciousness, language, and perceptual representation of the world.

The third line of discovery was the elucidation of neurochemical processes that underlie the orderly conduct of the various anatomical units of the brain (Crick, 1994). It is believed that abstract thought and even patterns of morality are organized in the frontal/cortical regions of the brain. Language appears to be lateralized in the left side of the brain (usually), while spatial and non-verbal functions reside in the right half of the brain. Similarly, we are acquiring a broader and deeper understanding of attention, learning, motivation, and consciousness. Day by day the neurophysiologists are unfolding the processes of the brain for our inspection.

The overriding principle that emerges from all of these investigations is that the brain is highly specialized, with functions localized in discrete areas of the brain, and with behaviors and consciousness under direct control of genes, neurons and specific experiences. There is nothing among these findings to support the suggestions that we have freed ourselves from the restraints of the past. Our behaviors are of course complex and often seem unpredictable and novel, but they are not independent of our evolutionary history.

There is a growing recognition that the brain and its functions are an extension of motor activity (Sheets-Johnstone, 1990). Apparently, movement and the encountering of the organism with its environment, forced the brain to evolve corresponding mental concepts about that environment. The evolution of movement skills brought with it perceptions and cognitive development. For example, recognition of up/down, front/

back, near/far may be neurological analogies of body movement in space. Similarly, the evolution of language in the left hemisphere of the brain may be the consequence of left/right differences in reaching and stabilizing the body. Asymmetrical movement in space may act to differentiate the brain for specialized skills involved in language (MacNeilage, 1994). Infant development may present the best evidence for motor control of cognitive development. Concepts dealing with space and relations among objects do not develop without interaction with the environment (Piaget, 1970). While these notions are complex (and incomplete), the suggestions are strong that motor behavior and mental functions are tightly linked.

Obviously the ancients knew little of this, sometimes confusing the functions of the brain with that of the heart, or even separating the body entirely from the "spiritual qualities of the mind." But what they and many others have realized since is that the brain is the seat of both "good" and "bad", definitely a mixed blessing. We rush across the landscape using the power of the brain, but we also suffer the consequences of our own evolutionary successes.

Some basic truths have been known for centuries—truths acquired through thought and self-examination, many still undeciphered by scientists. Among these are (1) mind and body are inseparable, (2) our creativity is the outcome of evolutionary history, inherited from parents to offspring, (3) social achievements rest on the complexity of our intellect, and most important, (4) we can never escape the "triune" nature of the brain. All thought, all action are motivated by primitive aspects of the brain constructed through evolution like piers that hold up the scaffolding of creativity and our darker side.

The Mixed Blessings of the Mind

Evolved Genius

We evolved a large, complex brain that unleashed our inner nature and propelled us toward language, art, politics, and science. Compared to other species we possess an unparalleled intellectual capacity. Often a blessing, still at other times it is a constraint of our other drives, making us most uncomfortable.

All genius is a conquering of chaos and mystery.

Otto Weininger
Austrian writer

All men by nature desire to know. ...we do not know a truth without knowing its cause.

Aristotle
Greek philosopher

No, what it [my mind] is really most like is a spider's web, insecurely hung on leaves and twigs, quivering in every wind, and sprinkled with dewdrops and dead flies. And at its geometric centre, pondering forever the Problem of Existence, sits motionless and spider-like, the uncanny Soul.

Logan Pearsall Smith
English scholar

There are mistakes that are creative.

Paul Valéry
French poet

A moment's insight is sometimes worth a life's experience.

Oliver Wendell Holmes
Supreme Court Justice

Imagination and fiction make up more than three quarters of our real life.

Simone Weil
French philosopher

Mind is ever the ruler of the universe.

Plato
Greek philosopher

By words the mind is winged.

Aristophanes
Athenian poet

Language is a part of our organism and no less complicated than it.

Ludwig Wittgenstein
Austrian philosopher

Language is the archives of history.

Ralph Waldo Emerson
American poet

Man is only a reed, the weakest in nature; but he is a thinking reed. There is no need for the whole universe to take up arms to crush him: a vapor, a drop of water is enough to kill him. But even if the universe were to crush him, man would still be nobler than his slayer, because he knows that he is dying and the advantage the universe has over him. The universe knows nothing of this.

Blaise Pascal
French philosopher

As long as our brain is a mystery, the universe, the reflection of the structure of the brain, will also be a mystery.

Santiago Ramón Cajal
Spanish scientist and philosopher

The unconscious is the ocean of the unsayable, of what has been expelled from the land of language, removed as a result of ancient prohibitions.

Italo Calvino
Italian author

Death is the price paid by life for an enhancement of the complexity of a live organism's structure.

Arnold Toynbee
British historian

I never heard tell of any clever man that came of entirely stupid people.

Thomas Carlyle
Scottish historian

To have the sense of creative activity is the great happiness and the great proof of being alive.

Matthew Arnold
British poet

The highest intellects, like the tops of mountains, are the first to catch and to reflect the dawn.

Lord Macaulay
British historian

There is one radical distinction between different minds... that some minds are stronger and apter to mark the differences of things, others to mark their resemblances.

Francis Bacon
English philosopher

On earth there is nothing great but man; in man there is nothing great but mind.

Sir William Hamilton
Socttish philosopher

A moment's insight is sometimes worth a life's experience.

Oliver Wendell Holmes
Supreme Court Justice

To create is divine, to reproduce is human.

Man Ray
American photographer

All the lies and evasions by which man has nourished himself—*civilization*, in a word—are the fruits of the creative artist. It is the creative nature of man which has refused to let him lapse back into that unconscious unity with life which characterizes the animal world from which he made his escape.

Henry Miller
American author

True creativity often starts where language ends.

Arthur Koestler
British novelist

Everything vanishes around me, and works are born as if out of a void. Ripe, graphic fruits fall off. My hand has become the obedient instrument of a remote will.

Paul Klee
Swiss artist

Make visible what, without you, might perhaps never have been seen.

Robert Bresson
French film director

The world embarrasses me, and I cannot dream that this watch exists and has no watchmaker.

Voltaire
French philosopher

Our inventions mirror our secret wishes.

Lawrence Durrell
Anglo-Irish novelist

Movement Underlies Intelligence

Despite past philosophic errors separating mind and body, we now know better. The mind is the brain in action; the brain is an organ of the body. Body, action, and thinking flow along identical biological conduits.

The body is an instrument, the mind its function, the witness and regard of its operation.

George Santayana
American philosopher

What we have to learn to do, we learn by doing.

Aristotle
Greek philosopher

There is more wisdom in your body than in your deepest philosophy.

Friedrich Nietzsche
German philosopher

Without the body, the soul is nothing but empty wind. Without the soul, the body is but a senseless frame.

Kahlil Gibran
Lebanese poet

From a man's face, I can read his character; if I can see him walk, I know his thoughts.

Petronius
Roman writer

The brain has muscles for thinking as the legs have muscles for walking.

Julien Offroy de la Mettrie
French philosopher

The features of our face are hardly more than gestures which force of habit made permanent. Nature, like the destruction of Pompeii, like the metamorphosis of a nymph into a tree, has arrested us in an accustomed movement.

Marcel Proust
French novelist

The mind grows and decays with the body.

Lucretius
Roman poet

Diseases of the mind impair the power of the body.

Lucretius
Roman poet

The Other Side of the Mental Coin

The brain can stifle the expression of basic attributes, sometimes acting to prevent the natural flow of basic drives into creative expression. Thinking can sometimes be dangerous, cutting us off from instinctive behaviors, and even leading us toward species extinction. Have we become too smart?

The brain is not an organ to be relied upon. It is developing monstrously. It is swelling like a goitre.

Aleksandr Blok
Russian poet

The mind is the most capricious of insects—flitting, fluttering.

Virginia Woolf
English novelist

Don't think! Thinking is the enemy of creativity. It's self-conscious, and anything self-conscious is lousy. You can't try to do things; you simply must do them.

Ray Bradbury
American author

It is wrong to think that misfortunes come from the east or from the west; they originate within one's own mind. Therefore, it is foolish to guard against misfortunes from the external world and leave the inner mind uncontrolled.

Seo Kyung Bo
Oriental philosopher

If you can engage people's pride, love, pity, ambition (or whatever is their prevailing passion) on your side, you need not fear what their reason can do against you.

Lord Chesterfield
English statesman

The more you reason the less you create.

Raymond Chandler
American novelist

I was taught that the human brain was the crowning glory of evolution so far, but I think it's a very poor scheme for survival.

Kurt Vonnegut, Jr.
American novelist

That priceless galaxy of misinformation called the mind.

Djuna Barnes
American novelist

Man is an over-complicated organism. If he is doomed to extinction he will die out for want of simplicity.

Ezra Pound
American poet

I see mysteries and complications wherever I look, and I have never met a steadily logical person.

Martha Gellhorn
American journalist

For in much wisdom is much grief: and he that increaseth knowledge increaseth sorrow.

Bible: Ecclesiastes 1: 18

The remarkable thing about the human mind is its range of limitations.

Celia Green
Feminist spokesperson

From ignorance our comfort flows. Only the wretched are the wise.

Matthew Prior
British poet

The emergence of intelligence, I am convinced, tends to unbalance the ecology. In other words, intelligence is the great polluter. It is not until a creature begins to manage its environment that nature is thrown into disorder.

Clifford D. Simak
American writer

Riches, Fame, and Pleasure. With these three the mind is so engrossed that it can hardly think of any other good.

Benedict Spinoza
Dutch philosopher

Man is an intelligence, not served by, but in servitude to his organs.

Aldous Huxley
British author

Intelligence is not all that important in the exercise of power, and is often, in point of fact, useless.

Henry Kissinger
American secretary of state

The heart has its reasons which reason does not understand.

Blaise Pascal
French philosopher

The greatest intellectual capacities are only found in connection with a vehement and passionate will.

Arthur M. Schlesinger, Jr.
American historian

When a man begins to reason, he ceases to feel.

French proverb

All the unhappy marriages come from the husbands having brains.
What good are brains to a man? They only unsettle him.

P.G. Wodehouse
British novelist

The intellect is always fooled by the heart.

Francois, Duc de la Rochefoucauld
French writer

The brain may devise laws for the blood, but a hot temper leaps
over a cold decree.

William Shakespeare
English playwright

The sexual organs are the true seat of the will, of which the opposite pole is the brain.

Simone de Beauvoir
French novelist

It is impossible to love and be wise.

Francis Bacon
English philosopher

Better that a girl has beauty than brains because boys see better
than they think.

Unknown

Love is the triumph of imagination over intelligence.

H. L. Mencken
American critic

It is almost as if you were frantically constructing another world
while the world that you live in dissolves beneath your feet, and
that your survival depends on completing this construction at least
one second before the old habituation collapses.

Tennessee Williams
American dramatist

Our current obsession with creativity is the result of our continued striving for immortality in an era when most people no longer believe in an after-life.

Arianna Stassinopoulos
Greek author

A large and complex brain provided the power for our imagination, allowing us to analyze our own dilemma and shape the world around us. History underlies our creativity, suggesting that language was that species-specific trait that linked our communication system to creativity. Creativity was seen as heritable, passing from generation to generation, much like physical characteristics.

Evidently, members of the literary world also saw a downside to brain evolution. While the brain-stuff added to our creativity it also added to our wretchedness: creativity is manifest from brain complexity, but is also associated with increased powers to self-indulge and destroy. Said in Ecclesiastes (1:18): "For in much wisdom is much grief; and he that increaseth knowledge increaseth sorrow." The thought is seen again in John Milton's "Paradise Lost." The historical lesson is reverberating throughout our civilization and the halls of science.

5

The Historical Depth of Culture

Social scientists emphasize the learned components of culture. The famed sociologist Emile Durkheim set our view of culture early in this century when he said that only "…social facts can explain social facts." Accordingly, social questions can not be reduced to biological explanations. After all, the language we acquire, the artifacts we produce, the culture we embrace, are unique expressions of our social complexity.

This view prevailed, fully compatible with the human capability of changing his environment, the political ascendancy of Marxism, and the psychological principles of behaviorism. Humans and animals demonstrated great behavioral flexibility, responding to reward and punishment, showing little evidence of instincts. The argument seemed settled: humans did evolve, acquiring a brain so complex that man was able to step beyond his animal constraints.

Suspicions remained that at the bottom of our cultural forms are the universal adaptations of millennia past. Yes, our languages, artifacts, and social beliefs are learned, but the "rules" of language acquisition, the constraints of our cultural ambitions, and the cognitive and emotional structure of our various beliefs are expressions of earlier evolutionary adaptations. The frosting on the cake may vary in multiple ways, but the cake itself is the immutable product of earlier genetic mixing.

The evidence for the evolution of culture is strong. For one thing, there are attributes of culture that are invariant—universals (Brown, 1991; Thiessen, 1996). They differ in degree and quality of expression but they remain fundamentally the same, regardless of language, idiosyncratic beliefs, and cultural history. Among the hundreds of universals are rules of kinship interactions, laws of inheritance of wealth, formalized marriage, child care, and divorce, incest taboos, governmental organizations, courtship acts, aggression, neuromuscular and perceptual traits, religion, use of clothes and body adornment, rape, suicide, and murder. There are hundreds of universal traits that are common to us all and speak loudly of our single evolutionary history.

The strongest evidence for evolutionary influences on culture is our obsession for the preservation of individual genes through social interactions (Barash, 1977; Dawkins, 1976; Wilson, 1975) or through those with whom we share genes (Alexander, 1979). As Dawkins (1995) poetically expresses our history: "Since all organisms inherit all their genes from their ancestors, rather than from their ancestors' unsuccessful contemporaries, all organisms tend to possess successful genes. They have what it takes to become ancestors—and that means to survive and reproduce. This is why organisms tend to inherit genes with a propensity to build a well-designed machine—a body that actively works as if it is striving to become an ancestor. That is why birds are so good at flying, fish so good at swimming, monkeys so good at climbing, viruses so good at spreading. That is why we love life and love sex and love children. It is because we all, without a single exception, inherit all our genes from an unbroken line of successful ancestors." We survive not to build societies; rather, we build societies to facilitate survival.

Kinship is the glue holding individuals together within social systems. Close kin are favored over distant kin, kin are favored over non-kin. In addition, we have developed reciprocal exchange systems that benefit individuals who are not related (Trivers, 1972). These are systems based on the adage, "You scratch my back and I'll scratch yours." Individuals can gain from the application of this rule if they agree on the parameters of exchange, and if "cheaters" can be detected and punished. Thus, genetic success of our ancestors flowed through both kinship relations and reciprocal altruism. Culture is the means by which individuals interact to gain reproductive advantages.

Cheaters are not bizarre exceptions to the general altruistic tendencies of social systems. Indeed, they arise because of human advantages; they are equally a part of our evolutionary past. Imagine what it would be like if we all spoke our minds, without regard to consequence? Consider our tendencies to disguise our weaknesses and our eagerness to gain advantages. Could we survive without deceptions? Could we face reality without deceiving ourselves? The biological conclusion is that deception of others and deception of self are merely other adaptations evolved to create individual advantages in social interactions (Alexander, 1979).

Social scientists are resisting the evolutionary interpretation of culture, mainly through name-calling, but their battle runs uphill. Anthropologists John Tooby and Leda Cosmides (1992) insist that the social sciences have a weak cultural tree because they have no biological roots. Biology is providing those roots. But, as we will see, the notions developed by biologists have their ancestors in the history of our language. While their expression lacks the coherence and generality of today's theorizing, the seeds were planted early.

The Origins of Culture

The Individual Within Society

Know the individual and one can understand culture. Humans did evolve social strategies, but only for the purpose of extending individual advantages. Many, coming before us, understood this relation.

It is the individual only who is timeless. Societies, cultures, and civilizations—past and present—are often incomprehensible to outsiders, but the individual's hungers, anxieties, dreams, and preoccupations have remained unchanged through the millennia.

Eric Hoffer
American philosopher

Man is a social animal.

Benedict Spinoza
Dutch philosopher

Man was formed for society.

William Blackstone
British jurist

There is no such thing as society: there are individual men and women, and there are families.

Margaret Thatcher
British Prime Minister

Man is not a solitary animal, and so long as social life survives, self-realization cannot be the supreme principle of ethics.

Bertrand Russell
British philosopher

If any civilization is to survive, it is the morality of altruism that men have to reject.

Ayn Rand
American writer

Every major horror of history was committed in the name of an altruistic motive. Has any act of selfishness ever equaled the carnage perpetrated by disciples of altruism.

Ayn Rand
American writer

Common sense is judgment without reflection shared by an entire class, an entire nation, or the entire human race.

Giambattista Vico
Italian philosopher

A race of altruists is necessarily a race of slaves. A race of free men is necessarily a race of egoists.

Max Stirner
German writer

All disinterested kindness is inexplicable.

Arthur M. Schlesinger, Jr.
American historian

We go to gain a little patch of ground that hath in it no profit but the name.

William Shakespeare
English playwright

Whenever a friend succeeds a little something in me dies.

Gore Vidal
American novelist

We all have strength enough to endure the misfortune of others.

Francois, Duc de la Rochefoucauld
French moralist

As some day it may happen that a victim must be found, I've got a little list—I've got a little list. Of society offenders who might well be underground, and who never would be missed—who never would be missed!

W. S. Gilbert
British dramatist

Show me a good and gracious loser and I'll show you a failure.

Knute Rockne
American football coach

Every man alone is sincere. At the entrance of a second person, hypocrisy begins.

Ralph Waldo Emerson
American essayist

Men often compete with one another until the day they die; comradeship consists of rubbing shoulders jocularly with a competitor.

Edward Hoagland
American novelist

O you gods! Why do you make us love your goodly gifts, and snatch them straight away?

William Shakespeare
English playwright

Hell is oneself, hell is alone, the other figures in it merely projections. There is nothing to escape from and nothing to escape to. One is always alone.

T. S. Eliot
Anglo-American poet

However energetically society in general may strive to make all the citizens equal and alike, the personal pride of each individual will always make him try to escape the common level, and he will form some inequality somewhere to his own profit.

Alexis de Tocqueville
French philosopher

From time immemorial it has been repeated, with hypocrisy, that *men are equal*; and from time immemorial the most degrading and the most monstrous inequality ceaselessly weigh on the human race.

Pierre Sylvain Marechal
French poet

Future: That period of time in which our affairs prosper, our friends are true and our happiness is assured.

Ambrose Bierce
American writer and journalist

Live and let live.

Scottish proverb

Cultural Sadness

We share an ambivalence toward culture because we were selected for small-group living, not large-group interactions. Additionally, our individual characteristics clash with the demands of society: we are animals, first of all, often with a nature incompatible with civilization. The conflicts are evident in the writings of men and women.

And man has actually invented God...the marvel is that such an idea, the idea of the necessity of God, could enter the head of such a savage, vicious beast as man.

Fyodor Dostoyevski
Russian novelist

Our civilization is still in a middle stage, scarcely beast, in that it is no longer wholly guided by instinct, scarcely human, in that it is not yet wholly guided by reason.

Theodore Dreiser
American writer

Ambition, avarice, self-love, vanity, friendship, generosity, public spirit: these passions, mixed in various degrees, and distributed through society, have been, from the beginning of the world, and still are, the source of all actions and enterprises, which have ever been observed among mankind.

David Hume
Scottish philosopher

The contemporary woman's liberation drive toward a *decrease* in sexual differentiation to the extent that it is leading toward androgyny and unisexual values, implies a social and cultural deathwish and the end of civilization that endorses it. The scientific and historical records show that all the way from unicellular organisms to human beings, progress in evolution has been stimulated by an *increase* in *sexual differentiation.*

> *Amaury de Biencourt*
> *French historian*

To accomplish great things we must live as if we were never going to die.

> *Luc de Clapiers, Marquis de Vauvenargues*
> *French moralist*

Pavarotti: He has pushed the twilight back.

> *Mike Wallace*
> *American television journalist*

We double, triple, centruple our speed, but we shatter our nerves in the process, and are the same trousered apes at two thousand miles an hour as when we had legs.

> *Will and Ariel Durant*
> *American historians*

No society has been able to abolish human sadness, no political system can deliver us from the pain of living, from our fear of death, our thirst for the absolute. It is the human condition that directs the social condition, not vice versa.

> *Eugéne Ionesco*
> *French playwright*

The skylines lit up at dead of night, the airconditioning systems cooling empty hotels in the desert and artificial light in the middle of the day all have something both demented and admirable about them. The mindless luxury of a rich civilization, and yet of a civilization perhaps as scared to see the lights go out as was the hunter in his primitive night.

> *Jean Baudrillard*
> *French semiologist*

Ah, love, let us be true to one another. For the world, which seems to lie before us like a land of dreams. So various, so beautiful, so new, hath really neither joy, nor love, nor light, nor certitude, nor peace, nor help for pain; and we are here as on a darkling plain; swept with confused alarms of struggle and flight, where ignorant armies clash by night.

Matthew Arnold
British poet

Reciprocal Altruism

Dealing with genetic strangers is problematical, as it is easy to be taken advantage of. We can, however, establish principles of social interaction that benefit both the giver and receiver of altruistic acts, provided that we agree that it's a give-and-take relation. From the Greeks to the present we have understood this.

Do not that to thy neighbor that thou wouldst not suffer from him.

Pittacus of Lesbos
One of the Seven Sages of Greece

Do to others as I would they should do to me.

Plato
Greek philosopher

To do exactly as your neighbors do is the only sensible rule.

Emily Post
American hostess

Send your grain across the seas, and in time you will get a return.

Bible: Ecclesiastes: 11:1

Tsekung asked, "Is there one single word that can serve as a principle of conduct for life?" Confucius replied, "Perhaps the word 'reciprocity' (*sku*) will do. Do not do unto others what you do not want others to do unto you."

Confucius
Chinese philosopher

The man mindful of his reputation does not reveal his sadness.

Early Anglo-Saxon author

I detest everything which is not perfectly mutual.

Lord Byron
British poet

People must help one another; it is nature's law.

Jean de La Fontaine
French fabulist

Character is much easier kept than recovered.

Thomas Paine
American political writer

Reputation, reputation, reputation! O, I ha' lost my reputation, I ha' lost the immortal part of myself, and what remains is bestial.

William Shakespeare
English playwright

Too great a hurry to discharge an obligation is a kind of ingratitude.

Francois, Duc de La Rochefoucauld
French writer

The Beauty of Social Lies

Deception of self and deception of others is often a key to survival and reproduction. Perhaps deception is essential, accounting for its universality and its perfect understanding by historians of man.

Nothing is so easy as to deceive one's self; for what we wish, we readily believe.

Demosthenes
Athenian orator

Every mind has a choice between truth and repose. Take which you please—you can never have both.

Ralph Waldo Emerson
American poet

But there are other things which a man is afraid to tell even to himself, and every decent man has a number of such things stored away in his mind... A man's true autobiography is almost an impossibility...man is bound to lie about himself.

Fyodor Dostoyevski
Russian novelist

Lies are essential to humanity. They are perhaps as important as the pursuit of pleasure and moreover are dictated by that pursuit.

Marcel Proust
French novelist

We lie loudest when we lie to ourselves.

Eric Hoffer
American philosopher

Nothing is so difficult as not deceiving ourself.

Ludwig Wittgenstein
Austrian philosopher

As a rule people are afraid of the truth. Each truth we discover in nature or social life destroys the crutches on which we need to lean.

Ernst Toller
German playwright

Look like the innocent flower, but be the serpent under it.

William Shakespeare
English playwright

A goodly apple rotten at the heart. O what a goodly outside false-hood hath!

William Shakespeare
English playwright

False face must hide what the false heart doth know.

William Shakespeare
English playwright

Lord, Lord, how this world is given to lying! I grant you I was down and out of breath; and so was he; but we rose both at an instant and fought a long hour by Shrewsbury clock.

William Shakespeare
English playwright

There is nothing like desire for preventing the thing one says from bearing any resemblance to what one has in mind.

Marcel Proust
French novelist

Every individual...intends only his own gain, and he is in this, as in many other cases, led by an invisible hand to promote an end which was no part of his intention...By pursuing his own interest he frequently promotes that of the society more effectively than when he really intends to promote it. I have never known much good done by those who affected to trade for the public good.

Adam Smith
Scottish economist

Too much *Truth* is uncouth.

Franklin P. Adams
American journalist

Almost every man wastes part of his life in attempts to display qualities which he does not possess, and to gain applause which he cannot keep.

Samuel Johnson
English writer

The true use of speech is not so much to express our wants as to conceal them.

Oliver Goldsmith
English writer

Lying increases the creative faculties, expands the ego, lessens the friction of social contacts... It is only in lies, wholeheartedly, and bravely told, that human nature attains through words and speech the forbearance, the nobility, the romance, the idealism, that—being what it is—it falls short of in fact and in deed.

Clare Boothe Luce
American diplomat

A little inaccuracy sometimes saves tons of explanation.

Saki (H. H. Munro)
British author

What does the truth matter? Haven't we mothers all given our sons a taste for lies, lies which from the cradle upwards lull them, reassure them, send them to sleep: lies as soft and warm as a breast.

Georges Bernanos
French novelist

Adults find pleasure in deceiving a child. They consider it necessary, but they also enjoy it. The children very quickly figure it out then practice deception themselves.

Elias Canetti
Austrian novelist

Our systems, perhaps, are nothing more than an unconscious apology for our faults—a gigantic scaffolding whose object is to hide from us our favorite sin.

Henri-Frédéric Amiel
Swiss philosopher

Of course I lie to people. But I lie altruistically—for our mutual good. The lie is the basic building blocks of good manners. That may seem mildly shocking to a moralist—but then what isn't.

Quentin Crisp
British author

I want my attorney, my tailor, my servants, even my wife, to believe in God, and I think that then I shall be robbed and cuckolded less often.

Voltaire
French philosopher

Natural selection does not select for societies; it selects for social traits in individuals that allow them advantages through social interactions. We are biased toward kin who share genes in common, and toward others who reciprocate good deeds. Thus, kin selection and reciprocal altruism lie at the basis of social systems. Without them there would be no cooperation and no culture.

Our social dispositions are written in the DNA of reproduction, giving us all universal traits that generally work well, regardless of learned artifacts of particular cultures. It is as if we have a limited range of social strategies that are adjusted according to the specific characteristics of our cultures. Cultural artifacts provide the learned rewards and punishments around which our universal traits circle.

There are downsides to cultures, in that compromises must always be made in order to extend our personal reproductive strategies. It's a matter of cost/benefit relations, where we attempt to optimize our genetic goals in a highly complex environment. We do what we must— reciprocate good deeds, lie to advance our cause, and deceive where necessary. The mix of traits is complex, reflecting our big brain capacities, and our indirect strategies for optimizing advantages. We never evolved to live in large societies, having a background of hunters and gatherers, but we do have the unusual capacity to extend our historical adaptations to uncommon situations.

6

Creativity and the Pain of Self-Discovery

Diseases of the mind and body weave through our evolutionary history. Some we understand; others we don't. Diseases caused by protozoa, bacteria, and viruses direct much of our defensive efforts and may be responsible for a great deal of our physiology and behavior (Ewald, 1994; Nesse & Williams, 1994). Still, our attempts to understand diseases of the body seem to fade in significance when contrasted to man's continual battle with his own psyche. Mental aberrations, light as a breeze or heavy as a hurricane, blow across our lives with disconcerting regularity.

Sometimes, deviations of the brain cause a complete breakdown of the organism, but at other times mental disease and creativity combine in unusual ways. Once when Karl Gauss was trying to solve an unusually perplexing mathematical problem, a servant told him that is ill wife was about to die. His only response: "Tell her to wait a moment 'til I'm through." The euphoria of creativity may have elevated his thinking, but it interfered with his life as a family man. We know little about peculiar combinations of traits, but they do open up special roads into the strange nature of the brain. Far more today than yesterday, biologists are concerned with irrationality and its links to creative genius.

Genius and insanity mix in proportionate amounts, giving validity to the notion that creativity often bubbles forth from madness. Researcher Kay Jamison (1995) indicates that scores of 18th, 19th and 20th century poets, artists, and writers suffered from periodic moods of depression and mania. Among these were William Blake, Lord Byron, Alfred Lord Tennyson, Sylvia Plath, Vincent van Gogh, Edgar Allan Poe, Virginia Woolf, Gustav Mahler, Ernest Hemingway, and many others. Most of these influential geniuses suffered from manic-depressive illness, or major depression. Even Aristotle wondered: "Why is that all men who are outstanding in philosophy, poetry, or the arts are melancholic?"

Intense mood swings show a strong genetic influence, moving down family pedigrees in patterns consistent with inherited factors. Alfred Lord Tennyson, who asserted that, "Science grows and beauty dwindles," was one of those blessed and burdened by family genes. His grandfather, two of his great-grandfathers, as well as five of his seven brothers suffered from insanity, melancholia, uncontrolled rage, or manic-depressive illness. All of these emotional states are known to be heavily influenced by genes.

The rates of manic-depressive illnesses and major depression are much higher among artists of all sorts than in the general population. Artists also experience up to 18 times the rate of suicide seen among other groups. Psychologist David Cohen emphasizes the genetic influence in this way: "Much of the relevant research, though not all, supports the idea that creative people in literature and the arts, as well as their biological relatives, tend to have mood swings, manic-depressive illness, and addictions. For example, a relatively high percentage of prize-winning or otherwise eminent writers, artists, and their close relatives have been found to be troubled by diagnosable mental illness. In seven family studies, from five to 70 percent of artists, writers, and poets were found to suffer depression and/or manic-depressive mood swing and to be at greater risk for suicide. Additional evidence comes from adoption research suggesting that the close biological (but not adoptive) relatives of especially creative adoptees have an elevated rate of depression, mood swing, alcohol problems, and personality disorders."

No one knows why creativity and mood disorders are associated. Certainly the majority of people who suffer from episodes of mania or hypomania (mild mania) or depression rarely show any signs of special creativity or insight. On the other hand, creative scientists do not seem extraordinary in their levels of affective disorders. Perhaps greater levels of rationality and cooperation are needed to be a scientist. But among artists who do suffer, the dark and light sides of mood-swings synergize into strange and unpredictable dimensions. Manic or hypomanic states elevate mood and feelings of self-esteem. Sleep becomes less necessary, speech becomes more rapid and excitable, and thoughts speed from one topic to another. During these times, especially, new ideas emerge and new creative horizons are crossed. It's as if a change in emotional state disturbs the brain's equilibrium, sending thoughts in totally new directions.

Unfortunately, manics and hypomanics generally lead chaotic lives. They fight mental demons on levels unknown to most of us, indulging in drugs, alcohol, hypersexuality, and ruthless interactions with others. The forces that elevate the mind to new levels of creativity are the same that send the mind careening along paths of self-destruction and degradation of others.

Depression is often the other side of the creative coin, where individuals become lethargic, lose concentration, and wallow in the lagoons of guilt, self-blame, and hopelessness. Suicide is common. But even depression may be a source of creativity, at least if it reverses and doesn't lead to self-destruction. Psychologist David Cohen (1994) argues that depressed individuals see the world with damnable realism. Cohen concludes: "With deepening depression comes a shifting mixture of certain kinds of abnormal thinking. One, depressive negativity, is a Hobbesian vision of the world as alien, hostile, uncontrollable, and of human life as solitary, poor, nasty, brutish, and short. The other, depressive realism, can mean just an absence of the usual positive bias. It can also mean an extraordinary ability to see objectively—what Byron called a 'fearful gift;' "…what is it but the telescope of truth which strips the distance of its fantasies and brings life near in utter nakedness, making the cold reality too real!" With an absence of defensive illusions and self-deception the indifferent world shows its true colors. Insights gained during intense depression may reemerge at a later time when they can be creatively communicated to others.

There are degrees of madness and creativity that most of us recognize, sometimes in ourselves. The genes do strange things at times, especially in certain environments. Madness is not always the consequence, as moods travel in many circles, aided and abetted by DNA. Homosexuality, personality characteristics, criminality, love, hate, and indifference ride the genetic waves. We are just beginning to understand the emotional make-up of man, expressed with deep insight by many who traveled these roads long ago. The irony is that many of the most creative people in history understood their own dilemma only because of the demons they fought.

Disease, Creativity, Madness, and Variations

Diseases of the Mind and Body

The general explanation of our evolution is that we adapted to a host of environmental changes. In its specific form, we adapted to climate, food supplies, predators, kin, strangers, and diseases of the body and mind. Many adaptations represent compromises among competing demands. Several writers were aware of our complicated nature.

The diseases which destroy a man are no less natural than the instincts which preserve him.

George Santayana
American philosopher

Think of the earth as a living organism that is being attacked by billions of bacteria whose numbers double every forty years. Either the host dies, or the virus dies, or both die.

Gore Vidal
American novelist

Diseased nature oftentimes breaks forth in strange eruptions.

William Shakespeare
English playwright

So, naturalist observe, a flea hath smaller fleas that on him prey. And these have smaller fleas to bite 'em. And so proceed *ad infinitum*.

Jonathan Swift
Anglo-Irish churchman and writer

Disease creates poverty and poverty disease. The vicious circle is closed.

Henry E. Sigerist
Medical historian

Happiness is beneficial for the body, but it is grief that develops the powers of the mind.

Marcel Proust
French novelist

Hope is necessary in every condition. The miseries of poverty, sickness, of captivity, would, without this comfort, be insupportable.

Samuel Johnson
English writer

The art of medicine consists of amusing the patient while Nature cures the disease.

Voltaire
French philosopher

The human body is the best picture of the human soul.

Ludwig Wittgenstein
Austrian philosopher

There are more microbes per person than the entire population of the world. Imagine that. Per person. This means that if the time scale is diminished in proportion to that of space it would be quite possible for the whole story of Greece and Rome to be played out between farts.

Alan Bennett
British dramatist

The Pain and Gain of Living

Life comes in opposites, joy and pain, love and hate, altruism and selfishness. That's the way it is; that's the way it always has been.

...we could never learn to be brave and patient if there were only joy in the world.

Helen Keller
American writer and lecturer

It is no good casting out devils. They belong to us, we must accept them and be at peace with them.

D. H. Lawrence
British novelist

For there was never yet a philosopher that could endure the toothache patiently.

William Shakespeare
English playwright

Take the life-lie away from the average man and straight away you take away his happiness.

Henrik Ibsen
Norwegian dramatist

Those who restrain Desire, do so because their's weak enough to be restrained.

William Blake
British poet

Nothing happens to any man that he is not formed by nature to bear.

Marcus Aurelius
Roman emperor

What does it mean for a painter to paint in the manner of So-and-So or to actually imitate someone else? What's wrong with that? On the contrary, it's a good idea. You should constantly try to paint like someone else. But the thing is, you can't! You would like to. You try. But it turns out to be a botch... And it's at the very moment you make a botch of it that you're yourself.

Pablo Picasso
Spanish painter

It is worth mentioning, for future reference, that the creative power which bubbles so pleasantly in beginning a new book quiets down after a time, and one goes on more steadily. Doubts creep in. Then one becomes resigned. Determination not to give in, and the sense of an impending shape keep one at it more than anything.

Virginia Woolf
British writer

The Creative Force of Madness

Creativity and madness are often tightly linked. We may not understand it, but we have noted it repeatedly.

Men have called me mad; but the question is not yet settled, whether madness is or is not the loftiest intelligence—whether much that is glorious—whether all that is profound—does not spring from disease of thought—from *moods* of mind exalted at the expense of the general intellect.

Edgar Allen Poe
American poet and writer

This story, "The Judgement," I wrote at one sitting during the night of 22nd-23rd, from ten o'clock at night to six o'clock in the morning. I was hardly able to pull my legs out from under the desk, they had got so stiff... The fearful strain and joy, how the story developed before me, as if I were advancing over water...How everything can be said, how for everything, for the strangest fancies there awaits a great fire in which they perish and rise up again... Only in this way can writing be done, only with such coherence, with such a complete opening out of the body and soul.

Franz Kafka
Czech novelist

Schizophrenic behaviour is a special strategy that a person invents in order to live in an unlivable situation.

R. D. Laing
British psychiatrist

Love is a grave mental disease.

Plato
Greek philosopher

Painting and sculpture, labour and good faith, have been my ruin and I continually go from bad to worse. Better would it have been for me if I had set myself to making matches in my youth. I should not be in such distress...

Michelangelo Buonarroti
Italian artist

For art to exist, for any sort of aesthetic activity or perception to exist, a certain physiological precondition is indispensable: intoxication.

Friedrich Nietzsche
German philosopher

As soon as he ceased to be mad he became merely stupid. There are maladies we must not seek to cure because they alone protect us from others that are more serious.

Marcel Proust
French novelist

The mass of mankind is divided into two classes, the Sancho Panzas who have a sense for reality, but no ideals, and the Don Quixotes with a sense for ideals, but mad.

George Santayana
American philosopher

Madness need not be all breakdown. It may also be breakthrough. It is potential liberation and renewal as well as enslavement and existential death.

R. D. Laing
British psychiatrist

There was never a genius without a tincture of madness.

Aristotle
Greek philosopher

Ordinarily he is insane, but he has lucid moments when he is only stupid.

Heinrich Heine
German poet

For me insanity is super-sanity. The normal is psychotic—a collective psychosis. Normal means lack of imagination, lack of creativity.

Jean Dubuffet
French painter

Take care your worship, those things over there are not giants but windmills.

Miguel de Cervantes
Spanish writer

I shudder and I sigh to think that even Cicero and many-minded Homer were *mad as the mist and snow*.

W. B. Yeats
Irish poet

The world has always gone through periods of madness so as to advance a bit on the road to reason.

Hermann Broch
Austrian novelist

Madness is part of all of us, all the time, and it comes and goes, waxes and wanes.

Otto Friedrich
American writer

Madness in great ones must not unwatch'd go.

William Shakespeare
English playwright

Self-Destruction as the Final Statement

Suicide is a human-typical behavior, sometimes related to psychological depression, occasionally provoked by situational demands. Some have said that suicide is *the* question of philosophy. Perhaps it is also a question of biology.

He that cuts off twenty years of life cuts off so many years of fearing death.

William Shakespeare
English playwright

There is but one truly serious philosophical problem and that is suicide. Judging whether life is or is not worth living amounts to answering the fundamental question of philosophy. All the rest— whether the mind has nine or twelve categories—comes afterwards. These are games; one must first answer.

Albert Camus
French writer

I have of late, but wherefore I know not, lost all my mirth, forgone all custom of exercises; and indeed, it goes so heavily with my disposition that this goodly frame, the earth, seems to me a sterile promontory; this most excellent canopy, the air, look you, this brave o'erhanging firmament, this majestical roof fretted with golden fire: why, it appeareth nothing to me but a foul pestilent congregation of vapors.

William Shakespeare
English playwright

The thought of suicide is great consolation: with the help of it, one has got through many a bad night.

Friedrich Nietzsche
German philosopher

Whom the gods would destroy, they first make mad.

Euripides
Greek dramatist

My work is done. Why wait?

George Eastman
American inventor

I take it that no man is educated who has never dallied with the thought of suicide.

William James
American writer

To be, or not to be—that is the question: Whether 'tis nobler in the mind to suffer the slings and arrows of outrageous fortune or to take arms against a sea of troubles, and by opposing end them. To die—to sleep—no more; and by a sleep to say we end the heartache, and the thousand natural shocks that flesh is heir to. 'Tis a consummation devoutly to be wish'd. To die—to sleep. To sleep—perchance to dream: ay, there's the rub! For in that sleep of death what dreams may come when we have shuffled off this mortal coil, must give us pause.

William Shakespeare
English playwright

Razors pain you;
Rivers are damp;
Acids stain you;
and drugs cause cramp.
Guns aren't lawful;
Nooses give;
Gas smells awful;
You might as well live.

Dorothy Parker
American humorist

Looking at Our Own Sexual Orientation

Homosexuality is considered by some a social deviation, and biologists would agree that nonreproductive behaviors are enigmas. Some would argue that variations in sexual orientations are correlated with creativity, but for others it is a burden. We know so little. Homosexuality may have a genetic and physiological basis. Beyond that statement we know little. There is little evidence that early rearing experiences are significant.

In homosexual sex you know exactly what the other person is feeling, so you are identifying with the other person completely. In heterosexual sex you have no idea what the other person is feeling.

> *William Burroughs*
> *American author*

Gay men may seek sex without emotion; lesbians often end up in emotion without sex.

> *Camille Paglia*
> *American author and educator*

There is probably no sensitive heterosexual alive who is not preoccupied with his latent homosexuality.

> *Norman Mailer*
> *American author*

We are not trying to imitate women.

> *Tennessee Williams*
> *American author*

Splendid couple—slept with both of them.

> *Maurice Bowra*
> *British academic*

Bisexuality immediately doubles your chances for a date on Saturday night.

> *Woody Allen*
> *American film director*

Humans have always had to cope with physical and mental diseases. In fact, diseases of the body and mind may have been two of the strongest selection forces in nature. Coping with disease may be one of the responses leading to increased brain flexibility and creativity. A complicated brain often offers solutions to ecological problems.

Creativity is not just a human trait, but it does express itself to the highest degree among humans. Many of our social qualities flow from individual creativity.

The problem is that creativity is a two-edged sword. It unleashes advantages that can increase survival and reproduction, but it also leads to dissatisfactions and, for little-known reasons in some, madness, depression, and suicide. For whatever reasons, creativity and discontent often tend to be married.

Other human deviations, such as homosexuality, are equally difficult to understand. Observations suggest that sexual orientation is strongly genetic in origin, but we know little about its underlying mechanisms. Variations in hormones, especially in early development, and possibly structural differences in the brain, may tell us something about these deviations.

7

Masters of Death

Biologists have long been interested in human aggression, but only recently has attention turned to biological issues of war and genocide (Daly & Wilson, 1986; Diamond, 1992; Green, 1991; Lopreato & Green, 1990). The study of the biology of human behavior is responsible for the shift, as this area of investigation offers evolutionary hypotheses for even the most devastating social behaviors. The attention given these broad social issues may prove to be critical in our understanding of human behavior.

Clearly our war-like behaviors are part of our evolutionary structure. However, as I said earlier (Thiessen, 1996), "It is simplistic to believe that we have specific genes for war, but we do have genes that predispose us to aggression, defensiveness, bonding, acquisition of resources, survival in face of danger, and reproduction. The traits are common to both sexes, but as usual they distribute themselves according to reproductive needs and, probably, testosterone levels. Men, more than women, band together, seek the thrill of battle, the stimulating fear of death, and the acknowledgment of survival and victory. Watch the fascination with war in the military, where statesmen, strategists, commanders, and troops swallow their fears and move to the fight. Watch the same motivations work themselves out with the male attachment to gang warfare, rough and tumble play, sports, driving, flying, video games, chess, business competition, and love relations. More than women, men are more concentrated, compelled, and competitive in war and their substitutes, forms of behavior entirely compatible with their polygynous style." Polygyny bred male competition, competition bred war. Anthropologist Irvin DeVore was once asked why men go to war? His answer was that "...the women are watching."

As man expanded his influence around the world he left millions of bodies in his wake. The greatest tragedies were not wars at all, but slaughters—genocides, with one group attempting to eliminate another. Since

1492, where records are available, hundreds of millions of people have been slaughtered by their aggressors (Diamond, 1992). The killers were European, Russian, Japanese, Spanish, Boers, Moslems, Hindus, African, Serbs, Muslins, Australians, and Turks. No one can avoid the "Mark of Cain;" no one can escape the wrath of his neighbor. Among the victims have been American and Caribbean Indians, Protestants, Catholics, Jews, Hindus, Moslems, Africans, European, Chinese, Serbs, and Tasmanians. The differences between killers and victims have nothing to do with geography, ethnicity, language, or religion. They have everything to do with human nature—greed, fear, suspicion, "we" verses "they." They have everything to do with expansionism and feelings of superiority.

Wars between nations seem almost tame by comparison. As nation-states formed, beginning around 1600, wars became formalized, fought by nations with specified rules of conduct (Clausewitz, 1976). Terrorism and genocide never vanished, however; it was cloaked in the rationale of nation wars, or conducted at the periphery of politics (Asprey, 1994).

Today, one can see that nation-states are crumbling into ethnic and political enclaves—smaller groups with clearer interests in common. The proliferation of selfish interests is ratcheting to new heights (Van Creveld, 1991; Weatherford, 1994). Joseph Motville at the Center for Strategic and International Studies in Washington D.C. believes that with the end of the cold war, groups with special interests were freer to act on ancient and new grievances. "It's as though the cops had gone home, and there's no one to answer 911." For the biologist, it's more like the veneer of civilization has been stripped away, revealing bare selfish genes.

Biologists are taking the rare step of suggesting that all selfish acts, from competition for resources to flat-out murder, are related to past adaptations for successful reproduction. Humans were never selected for pure, sacrificial altruism; they were selected for individual advantages in the struggle for life and reproduction. Murder, abuse, terrorism, genocide, revolution, and war are natural products of the evolution for reproductive advantages (Daly & Wilson, 1986; Green, 1991; Lopreato & Green, 1990). These are disturbing hypotheses about human existence, but not unlike those thoughts arising from our own history.

Death in Large Amounts

Our Basic Fascination for Evil

Evil is attractive: it draws our attention, stimulates the hormones, and roars with power. Evil may also be a natural design feature of our evolution. If true, then the word *evil* should be discarded from our language.

> Only those who know very little about the history of mankind can suppose that cruelty, crime or weakness, mass slaughter or mass corruption, are exceptions from the normal human rule. A doctrine of human nature that paints a picture of what might be that is in direct contradiction to what he has always and everywhere been may be a comfort to the spirit, but is not to be taken very seriously as a scientific hypothesis.
>
> *James Burnham*
> *American social philosopher*

> Must I do all the evil I can before I learn to shun it? Is it not enough to know the evil to shun it? If not, we should be sincere enough to admit that we love evil too well to give it up.
>
> *Mohandas K. Gandhi*
> *Indian spiritual leader*

> A great civilization is not conquered from without until it has destroyed itself from within. The essential cause of Rome's decline lay in her people, her morals, her class struggle, her failing trade, her bureaucratic despotism, her stifling taxes, her consuming wars...Rome was not destroyed by Christianity, any more than by barbarian invasion; it was an empty shell when Christianity arose to influence and invasion came.
>
> *Will Durant and Ariel Durant*
> *American historians*

> The exemption of women from military service is founded not on any natural inaptitude that men do not share, but on the fact that communities cannot reproduce themselves without plenty of women. Men are largely dispensable, and are sacrificed accordingly.
>
> *George Bernard Shaw*
> *Irish dramatist*

> The cannon thunders...limbs fly in all direction...one can hear the groans of victims and the howling of those performing the sacrifice...it's Humanity in search of happiness.
>
> *Charles Baudelaire*
> *French poet*

War will never cease until babies begin to come into the world with larger cerebrums and smaller adrenal glands.

H. L. Mencken
American political journalist

Man is insatiable for power; he is infantile in his desires and, always discontented with what he has, loves only what he has not. People complain of the despotism of princes; they ought to complain of the despotism of *man*.

Joseph de Maistre
French diplomat

Destruction, hence, like creation, is one of Nature's mandates.

Marquis de Sade
French author

But what experience and history teach is this—that peoples and governments have never learned anything from history, or acted on principles deduced from it.

Georg Wilhelm Friedrich Hegel
German philosopher

If you want to know the taste of a pear, you must change the pear by eating it yourself... If you want to know the theory and methods of revolution, you must take part in revolution. All genuine knowledge originates in direct experience.

Mao Tse-tung
Founder, People's Republic of China

Love of War

Every strategy to be successful must be painted with a hedonistic color; that is, each basic drive must have an emotional motivation behind it. Sex, to occur, must be exciting; feeding, to continue, must be satisfying; aggression, to survive, must be pleasant. And, what about war?

Let me have war, say I; it exceeds peace as far as day does night; it's sprightly, waking, audible, and full of vent. Peace is a very apoplexy, lethargy: mulled, deaf, sleepy, insensible; a getter of more bastard children than war's a destroyer of men.

William Shakespeare
English playwright

Man's greatest good fortune is to chase and defeat his enemy, seize his total possessions, leave his married women weeping and wailing, ride his gelding [and] use the bodies of his women as a nightshirt and support.

Genghis Khan
Mongolian warrior

They would rather be alive than free—them dumb bastards.

Dorian Harewood
American movie: Full Metal Jacket

I wanted to be the first person on my block to get a confirmed kill.

Matthew Modine
American movie: Full Metal Jacket

War is regarded as nothing but the continuations of politics by other means.

Karl von Clausewitz
Prussian soldier

The most persistent sound which reverberates through man's history is the beating of war drums.

Arthur Koestler
British novelist

War educates the senses, calls into action the will, perfects the physical constitution, brings men into sack swift and close collision in critical moments that men measures man.

Ralph Waldo Emerson
American essayist

Aggressiveness is the principal guarantor of survival.

Robert Ardrey
American writer

It isn't evil that is ruining the earth, but mediocrity. The crime is not that Nero played while Rome burned, but that he played badly.

Ned Rorem
American composer

The statistics of suicide show that, for non-combatants at least, life is more interesting in war than in peace.

Dean William Ralph Inge
British churchman

Everyone has observed how much more dogs are animated when they hunt in a pack, than when they pursue their game apart. We might, perhaps, be at a loss to explain this phenomenon, if we had not experience of a similar in ourselves.

David Hume
Scottish philosopher

For some men the power to destroy life becomes the equivalent to the female power to create life.

Myriam Miedzian
American author

A warlike spirit, which alone can create and civilize a state, is absolutely essential to national defense and to national perpetuity... The more warlike the spirit of the people, the less need for a large standing army... Every male brought into existence should be taught from infancy that the military service of the Republic carries with it honor and distinction, and his very life should be permeated with the ideal that even death itself may become a boon when a man dies that a nation may live and fulfill its destiny.

Douglas MacArthur
General of the U.S. Army

He butchered three of them with an ax and decapitated them. In other words, instead of using a gun to kill them he took a hatchet to chop their heads off. He struggled face to face with one of them, and throwing down his ax managed to break his neck and devour his flesh in front of his comrades...I...awarded him the Medal of the Republic.

General Mustafa T'las
Syrian minister of defense,
praising a 1973 hero of the war
with Israel before the Syrian
National Assembly

Cry "havoc!" and let loose the dogs of war, that this foul deed shall smell above the earth with carrion men, groaning for burial.

William Shakespeare
English playwright

The enemy advances: we retreat
The enemy halts: we harass
The enemy tires: we attack
The enemy retreats: we pursue

Mao Zedong
Founder, People's Republic of China

I love war... Peace will be hell for me.

George S. Patton, Jr.
American general

Personal Indifference, Hate, and Fear

Bricks can become a cathedral, as individual traits can rock a nation. One is not the other, however, as concepts must underlie the building of a cathedral or the construction of a nation. Facts and events are important, of course, but ideas are paramount. One can study the sociology of mass murder by war and genocide until the cows come home, but it will never be explained until the individual is known from all sides. One must have a concept of man.

If we take the generally accepted definition of bravery as a quality which knows no fear. I have never seen a brave man. All men are frightened. The more intelligent they are, the more they are frightened.

George S. Patton, Jr.
American general

We are all strong enough to bear the misfortunes of others.

Francois, Duc de la Rochefoucauld
French writer

Perish the Universe, provided I have my revenge.

Cyrano de Bergerac
French writer

The humble and meek are thirsting for blood.

Joe Orton
British dramatist

The least pain in our little finger gives us more concern and un-
easiness than the destruction of millions of our fellow-beings.

William Hazlitt
British essayist

One cannot weep for the entire world, it is beyond human strength.
One must choose.

Jean Anouilh
French playwright

This is the way the world ends, not with a bang but a whimper.

T. S. Eliot
Anglo-American poet

There is always inequality in life. Some are killed in war and
some men are wounded and some men never leave the country.
Life is unfair.

John F. Kennedy
American president

Conviction and Genocide

We rise to every occasion with the appropriate rationalization. Logic
is as logic will, meaning that we can justify anything, except injustice
to ourselves. Now there's the power of natural selection at the level of
the individual.

There is no instant of time when one creature is not being devoured
by another. Over all these numerous races of animals man is placed,
and his destructive hand spares nothing that lives. He kills to obtain
food and he kills to cloth himself; he kills to adorn himself; he kills
in order to attack and he kills to defend himself; he kills to instruct
himself and he kills to amuse himself; he kills to kill. Proud and
terrible king, he wants everything and nothing resists him.

Joseph de Maistre
French diplomat

The conquest of earth, which mostly means the taking it away from those who have a different complexion or simply flatter noses than ourselves, is not a pretty thing when you look into it.

Joseph Conrad
English novelist

Men never do evil so completely and cheerfully as when they do it from religious conviction.

Blaise Pascal
French philosopher

...the people imagine they are pursuing the Glory of God when actually they are only pursuing their own.

Blaise Pascal
French philosopher

And if any mischief follow, then thou shalt give life for life, eye for eye, tooth for tooth, hand for hand, foot for foot, burning for burning, wound for wound, stripe for stripe.

Bible: Exodus 21:23

The condition of man...is a condition of war of everyone against everyone.

Thomas Hobbes
British philosopher

Civilization is the lamb's skin in which barbarism masquerades.

Thomas Bailey Aldrich
American writer

Genocide begins, improbably, in the conviction that classes of biological distinction indisputably sanction social and political discrimination.

Andrea Dworkin
American feminist critic

Foremost leaders, dearest kinsmen, lying on the gory plain! "Lofty scorn of foes unworthy spared them from my flaming ire, but the blood of slaughtered kinsmen claims from me a vengence dire."

The Epic of Rama
Translated by Romesh Dutt

Let peace be sought through war.

Oliver Cromwell
English statesman and lord protector

Appeasing of governments which revel in slaughter is an invitation to worldwide catastrophe.

Fang Lizhi
Writer

I would suggest that barbarism be considered as a permanent and universal human characteristic which becomes more or less pronounced according to the play of circumstances.

Simone Weil
French philosopher

Let Rome in Tiber melt, and the wide arch of the ranged empire fall... The jungle is still the jungle, be it composed of trees or skyscrapers, and the law of the jungle is bite or be bitten.

George Lester Jackson
Writer

The Birth of Revolution

Nation-states are bound to pass; they rarely serve the interests of the individual, or the interests of various ethnic or religious groups. There is always the striving for social dominance and the acquisition of resources. For those reasons, governments are the genesis of revolution. Topple one government for another and watch the birth of a new revolution.

Insurrection—by means of guerrilla bands—is the true method of warfare for all nations desirous of emancipating themselves from a foreign yoke... It is invincible, indestructible.

Giuseppe Mazzini
Italian nationalist leader

All civilization has from time to time become a thin crust over a volcano of revolution.

Havelock Ellis
British psychologist

Revolution is delightful in the preliminary stages. So long as it's a question of getting rid of the people at the top.

Aldous Huxley
British writer

Inferiors revolt in order that they may be equal and equals that they may be superior. Such is the state of mind which creates revolutions.

Aristotle
Greek philosopher

What is wrong with a revolution is that it is natural. It is as natural as natural selection, as devastating as natural selection, and as horrible.

William Golding
British novelist

War and genocide—evil in large doses—are the natural outgrowth of the individual selfish gene. Individuals were designed to discriminate between allies and enemies, between gene similarities and gene differences. The "we" verses "they" distinction, valuable as it is in small groups, also sets groups apart, each with its special interests. The divisions may seem small but they set the stage for group and individual exploitation. War and genocide may follow.

The question, not yet solved by historians or scientists, is does the word *evil* apply in issues of war and genocide. If we believe that evil can be expunged through reinforcement or punishment, or if we believe that evil is learned, then the answer is probably yes. But if war and genocide are natural extensions of selfishness, aggression, and competition, then to call them evil is a value judgment about what is normal and abnormal. Take your pick.

8

Trying to Go Beyond the Genes

Natural selection leads us toward no particular end; it is an indifferent process that allows certain traits to survive, others to fail. It is a screening process akin to a sieve that permits some particles of sand through its pores, but not others. There is no great secret message in evolution, only a blind outcome of a ruthless sorting (Dawkins, 1986).

We are what we are, then—a product of a shifting history, the outcome of chance and circumstance (Gould, 1989). What we know of the world is a reflection of that—notions of chaos, feelings of past environmental influences, predispositions that saved our ancestors. This is the reservoir of our real knowledge, our species-specific character, our universal and unavoidable nature. Even what we learn and how we learn it is predetermined by the structure and significance of our past. We can learn any number of languages, or we can learn history, calculus, or bedtime stories, but how we learn them, how fast we can learn, and whether or not we retain information are all constrained by our evolutionary past and our individual genetic differences. The rules of learning and memory come down through the generations, only the text of life and how we see it varies from moment to moment.

Nevertheless, novelty does sometimes flow from evolutionary constraints, and new thoughts emerge from chaos (Gleick, 1987; Gutzwiller, 1992; Lewin, 1992; Prigogine & Stengers, 1984; Swinney, 1993). Yes, we are what our ancestors were, but individuals do differ and new traits do appear. David Lykken and his colleagues (1992) refer to the sudden appearance of uniqueness in offspring as *emergenesis*. What they mean is that some unusual gene combinations lead to a reorganization of traits that cannot be predicted by what happened in previous generations. The history of your family might be composed of "mathematical idiots," yet because of a novel combination of genes from you and your spouse, your daughter may

119

be a mathematical genius. There is no predicting this by looking at pedigrees, and there is little possibility that this ability will ever reappear in your grandchildren or great grandchildren.

Lykken and his associates point to the thoroughbred horse Secretariat as an example of emergenesis. The usual process of artificial selection had produced excellent thoroughbred racers, but most differences among horses were due to modest variations in training, nutrition, and veterinary techniques. "And then along came Secretariat, a great red stallion who lay down and took a nap on the day of his Kentucky Derby and then got up and broke the course record, not by just a whisker but by seconds. He did the same thing at Pimlico and then won the Belmont—and the Triple Crown—by more than 30 lengths. Put out at once to stud, where only the most promising mares could afford his fees, Secretariat sired more than 400 foals—most of them disappointments, none of them remotely in their sire's class. Secretariat had a distinguished lineage, of course, although none of his forebears could have run with him, but whatever he received at the great lottery of his conception could not be easily passed on in random halves. It seems a reasonable conjecture that Secretariat's qualities were configural [patterned], emergenic." And therein lies the promise of salvation from genetic determinism: if we harbor novelty and unpredictability are we not exceptions to the force of the genes?

But emergenic traits are not exceptions to the notion that causality is behind all structures—"this always leads to that"—but they do illustrate that not everything is predictable in terms of earlier adaptations. Individuals differ in unexpected ways. There is much we don't understand. There are also human traits that seem outside the range of genetic understanding, speaking softly of true altruism, free will, self-determination, and unusual courage in the face of near certain death (Thiessen, 1996). These traits may turn out to be no exception to those evolved for adaptive purposes, but for now we know little more than did the ancients.

Reaching for Star Stuff

Stark Reality

Facing reality is rough, like lying on a bed of nails rather than on down-stuffed pillows. Still, many poets, philosophers, and novelists did just that, many times over. Their thoughts are our treasures.

Imagine spending four billion years stocking the oceans with sea-food, filling the ground with fossil fuels, and drilling the bees in honey production—only to produce a race of bed-wetters!

Barbara Ehrenreich
American author

There is no doubt: the study of man is just beginning, at the same time that his end is in sight.

Elias Canetti
Austrian philosopher

The best history is but like the art of Rembrandt; it casts a vivid light on certain selected cases, on those which were best and greatest; it leaves all the rest in shadow and unseen.

Walter Bagehot
British economist

Some of us still get all weepy when we think about the Gaia Hypothesis, the idea that earth is a big furry goddess-creature who resembles everybody's mom in that she knows what's best for us. But if you look at the historical record—Krakatoa, Mt. Vesuvius, Hurricane Charley, poison ivy, and so forth down the ages—you have to ask yourself: Whose side is she on, anyway?

Barbara Ehrenreich
American author

Equality of opportunity means equal opportunity to be unequal.

Iain Macleod
British politician

Man's chief goal in life is still to become and stay human, and defend his achievements against the encroachment of nature.

Eric Hoffer
American philosopher

Compassion has no place in the natural order of the world which operates on the basis of necessity. Compassion opposes this order and is therefore best thought of as being in some way supernatural.

John Berger
British author

From an evolutionary point of view, man has stopped moving, if he ever did move.

Pierre Teilhard de Chardin
French Jesuit

How oft when men are at the point of death have they been merry! Romeo notes that jailers call this mood a "lightning before death."

William Shakespeare
English playwright

Between the idea and the reality, between the notion and the act falls the shadow.

T. S. Eliot
Anglo-American poet

Nothing certain exists, and...nothing is more pitiful or more presumptuous than man.

Pliny the Elder
Roman naturalist

No matter how cynical you become, you can't keep up.

George Will
American political commentator

Science grows and beauty dwindles.

Alfred Lord Tennyson
English poet

Inevitable Causes

Early writers constructed a philosophy by which science conducts its activities. It was a philosophy of empiricism, theory construction, and hypothesis testing. These common mental tools of science were pounded out long ago.

So free we seem, so fettered fast we are!

Robert Browning
English poet

Results are what you expect, and consequences are what you get.

Schoolgirl's comment on causality

True science teaches, above all, to doubt and to be ignorant.

Miguel de Unamuno
Spanish writer

I don't believe in accidents. There are only encounters in history. There are no accidents.

Elie Wiesel
American writer

The same motives always produce the same actions; the same events follow the same causes.

David Hume
Scottish philosopher

The doctrine of a first cause and the very idea of miracles vanish with the notion of causality.

Charles S. Peirce
American philosopher

The facts are to blame, my friend. We are all imprisoned by facts: I was born, I exist.

Luigi Pirandello
Italian dramatist

The facts speak for themselves.

Titus Maccius Plautus
Roman comic dramatist

The facts: nothing matters but the facts: worship of the facts leads to everything, to happiness first of all and then to wealth.

Edmond and Jules de Goncourt
French writers

Rose is a rose is a rose...

Gertrude Stein
American writer

Now what I want is, Facts... Facts alone are wanted in life.

Charles Dickens
English novelist

Do not become archivists of facts. Try to penetrate the secret of their occurrence, persistently search for the laws which govern them.

Ivan Pavlov
Russian Nobel laureate

Science is facts. Just as houses are made of stones, so is science made of facts. But a pile of stones is not a house and a collection of facts is not necessarily science.

Jules Henri Poincaré
French philosopher of science

Chance and Circumstance

Chance is a dreaded notion in biology, simply because science assumes that there are causes for every effect, predictable and lawful. This belief, or rather a hope, has been shattered by demonstrations of randomness and contingent processes. Perhaps everything is causal, but our view is short-sighted and blurred. All we know at this point, and have always realized, is that we operate within a biological lottery, our lives unpredictable, our lives making uncertain turns.

Traditional scientific method has always been at the very *best*, 20-20 hindsight. It's good for seeing where you've been.

Robert T. Pirsig
American writer

The slings and arrows of outrageous fortune.

William Shakespeare
English playwright

The giddy round of Fortune's wheel.

William Shakespeare
English playwright

Animals learn death first at the moment of death...man approaches death with the knowledge it is closer every hour, and this creates a feeling of uncertainty over his life, even for him who forgets in the business of life that annihilation is awaiting him. It is for this reason chiefly that we have philosophy and religion.

Arthur Schopenhauer
German philosopher

The grand Perhaps.

Robert Browning
English poet

Nothing exists per se except atoms and the void.

Lucretius
Greek philosopher

A chapter of accidents.

Earl of Chesterfield
English statesman

The present is never our goal; the past and present are our means; the future alone is our goal. Thus we never live but we hope to live; and always hoping to be happy, it is inevitable that we will never be so.

Blaise Pascal
French philosopher

If life were eternal all interest and anticipation would vanish. It is uncertainty which lends it satisfaction.

Kenkó Hoshi
Japanese Buddhist

Suddenly, as rare things will, it vanished.

Robert Browning
English poet

You could not step twice into the same rivers; for other waters are ever flowing on to you.

Heraclitus
Greek philosopher

Everything flows and nothing stays.

Heraclitus
Greek philosopher

All things change, nothing is extinguished... There is nothing in the whole world which is permanent. Everything flows onward; all things are brought into being with a changing nature; the ages themselves glide by in constant movement.

Ovid
Roman poet

It is seldom in life that one knows that a coming event is to be of crucial importance.

Anya Seton
American writer

How many things which served us yesterday as articles of faith, are fables for us today?

Michel de Montaigne
French philosopher

All great truths begin as blasphemies.

George Bernard Shaw
Irish dramatist

God...created a number of possibilities in case some of his prototypes failed—that is the meaning of evolution.

Graham Greene
British novelist

There is always something rather absurd about the past.

Max Beerbohm
British essayist

Nothing is inevitable until it happens.

A. J. P. Taylor
British historian

When one door shuts, another opens.

Proverb

Cleopatra's nose: if it had been shorter the face of the world would have been changed.

Blaise Pascal
French philosopher

Nothing is certain except the past.

Lucius Annaeus Seneca
Roman statesman

There's no limit to how complicated things can get, on account of one thing always leading to another.

E. B. White
American humorist

Accidental and fortuitous concurrence of atoms.

Lord Palmerston
British statesman

Better an ounce of luck than a pound of gold.

Yiddish proverb

In short, Luck's always to blame.

Jean de la Fontaine
French poet and fabulist

How sour sweet music is when time in broke and no proportion kept! So is it in the music of men's lives.

William Shakespeare
English playwright

Confusion is a word we have invented for an order which is not understood.

Henry Miller
American novelist

However well organized the foundations of life may be, life must always be full of risks.

Havelock Ellis
British psychologist

Today we were unlucky, but remember, we have only to be lucky once. You have to be lucky always.

Anonymous telephone tip
from IRA about attempt on
Margaret Thatcher's life

The sum of things is unlimited, and they all change into one another. The All includes the empty as well as the full. The worlds are formed when atoms fall into the void and are entangled with another; and from their motion as they increase in bulk, arises the substance of the stars.

Leucippus
Greek philosopher

Let us beware of saying there are laws in nature. There are only necessities: there is no one to command, no one to obey, no one to transgress. When you realize there are no goals or objectives, then you realize, too, that there is no chance: for only in a world of objectives does the word "chance" have any meaning.

Friedrich Nietzsche
German philosopher

There is not any present moment that is unconnected with some future one. The life of every man is a continued chain of incidents, each link of which hangs upon the former. The transition from cause to effect, from event to event, is often carried on by secret steps, which our foresight cannot divine, and our sagacity is unable to trace. Evil may at some future period bring forth good; and good may bring forth evil, both equally unexpected.

Joseph Addison
British essayist

I returned, and saw under the sun, that the race is not to the swift, nor the battle to the strong, neither yet bread to the wise, nor yet riches to men of understanding, nor yet favour to men of understanding, nor yet favour to men of skill; but time and chance happeneth to them all. For man also knoweth not his time: as the fishes that are taken in an evil net, and as birds that are caught in the snare; so are the sons of men snared in an evil time, when it falleth suddenly upon them.

Bible: Ecclesiastes 9: 11-12

Birth Out of Chaos

Chance wafts through our lives, seemingly making a mockery of laws of causation. Not true, of course; it's just that we have few measures of how chance operates. Occasionally, from out of a chaotic cauldron emerges the new and the unusual—order out of disorder.

I tell you: one must have chaos in one, to give birth to a dancing star. I tell you: yea have still chaos in you.

> *Frederick Nietzsche*
> *German philosopher*

Chaos is a name for any order that produces confusion in our minds.

> *George Santayana*
> *American philosopher*

Chaos often breeds life, when order breeds habit.

> *Henry Brooks Adams*

There are...intangible realities which float near us, formless and without words; realities which no one has thought out, and which are excluded for lack of interpreters.

> *Natalie Clifford Barney*
> *American author*

Error, like straws, upon the surface flow; he who would search for pearls must dive below.

> *John Dryden*
> *English poet*

Disorder is the condition of the mind's fertility; it contains the mind's promise, since its fertility depends upon the unexpected, it depends rather on what we do not know...than what we know.

> *Paul Valéry*
> *French poet*

Nothing arises in the body of order that we may use it, but what arises brings forth its own use... It was no design of the atoms that led them to arrange themselves in order with keen intelligence...but because many atoms in infinite time have moved and met in all manner of ways, trying all combination... Whence arose the beginnings of things...and the generation of living creatures.

Lucretius
Roman poet

Growing Through Enlightenment

The temptation is, of course, to divorce ourselves from reality, causation, and chance, turning within and separating ourselves from the environment. It has been done for thousands of years, yet we know little about how it works.

God is but a word invoked to explain the world.

Alphonse de Lamartine
French writer

Striving through satori—enlightenment meditation.

Zen Buddhism
Egoless

Back of every creation, supporting it like an arch, is faith. Enthusiasm is nothing: it comes and goes. But if one *believes*, then miracles occur.

Henry Miller
American author

The practitioners of Zen, ...has no fear of death, for he has annihilated himself so often. And he knows that in death...he will be annihilated, exalted, and preserved (as a field of power). Personal immortality has ceased to be a problem for him.

Eugen Herrigel
German author

Do "I" hit the goal, or does the goal hit me? Is "It" spiritual when seen by the eyes of the body, and corporeal when seen by the eyes of the spirit—or both or neither? Bow, arrow, goal and ego, all melt into one another, so that I can no longer separate them. And even the need to separate has gone. For as soon as I take the bow and shoot, everything becomes so clear and straightforward and so ridiculously simple.

Eugen Herrigel
German author

The Will to Survive

We hope, fantasize, and reach out for survival. The will to survive is paramount in the evolutionary game of reproduction. It must be considered the *first* adaptation.

People are inexterminable—like flies and bed-bugs. There will always be some that survive in cracks and crevices—that's us.

Robert Frost
American poet

The dogma of the Ghost in the Machine.

Gilbert Ryle
British philosopher

My sun sets to rise again.

Robert Browning
English poet

Even without the aid of artificial gadgetry human beings are able to survive and flourish in forests and in deserts, in the tropics and the Arctic...no other natural species has this kind of flexibility. So if man evolved from his predecessors by natural selection associated with adaptations to a specialized environment, what kind of environment was that?

Sir Edmund Leach
British author

Human beings *will* be happier—not when they cure cancer or get to Mars or eliminate racial prejudice or flush Lake Erie but when they find ways to inhabit primitive communities again. That's my utopia.

Kurt Vonnegut, Jr.
American novelist

Courage for Tomorrow

Always facing great odds, humans manage to cope, and even show great courage. It is the trait that characterizes the best in individuals—difficult to explain, but beautiful to behold.

That's one small step for man, one great leap for mankind.

Neil Armstrong
United States astronaut on the moon

What is passion? It is surely the becoming of a person. Are we not, for most of our lives, marking time? Most of our being is at rest, unlived. In passion, the body and the spirit seek expression outside of self. Passion is all that is other than self. Sex is only interesting when it releases passion. The more extreme and the more expressed that passion is, the more unbearable does life seem without it. It reminds us that if passion dies or is denied, we are partly dead and that soon, come what may, we will be wholly so.

John Boorman
British filmmaker

Passion, though a bad regulator, is a powerful spring.

Ralph Waldo Emerson
American essayist

There is in most passions a shrinking away from ourselves. The passionate pursuer has all the earmarks of a fugitive.

Eric Hoffer
American philosopher

There are two paths to take; one back toward comfort and security of death, the other forward to nowhere.

Henry Miller
American author

My candle burns at both ends; it will not last the night; but, ah, my foes, and oh, my friends—it gives a lovely light!

Edna St. Vincent Millay
American poet

Hope is the only universal liar who never loses his reputation for veracity.

Robert G. Ingersoll
American lawyer

Once one determines that he or she has a mission in life, that's it's not going to be accomplished without a great deal of pain, and that the rewards in the end may not outweigh the pain—if you recognize historically that that always happens, then when it comes, you survive it.

Richard Nixon
American president

It may be that the most interesting American struggle is the struggle to set oneself free from the limits one is born to, and then to learn something of the value of those limits.

Greil Marcus
American rock journalist

We are not now that strength which in old days moved earth and heaven; that which we are, we are; our equal temper of heroic hearts, made weak by time and fate, but strong in will to strive, to seek, to find, and not to yield.

Alfred Lord Tennyson
English poet

None but the brave deserves the fair.

John Dryden
English poet

It is better to be a widow of a hero than the wife of a coward.

Dolores Ibarruri
Spanish politician

Into the jaws of Death, into the mouth of Hell.

Alfred Lord Tennyson
English poet

Fortune favours the brave.

Terence
Roman poet

The hero is strangely akin to those who die young.

Rainer Maria Rilke
Austrian poet

And yet, hope pursues me, encircles me, bites me; like a dying wolf tightening his grip for the last time.

Frederico Garcia Lorca
Spanish poet

It is the perpetual dread of fear, *the fear of fear*, that shapes the face of a brave man.

Georges Bernanos
French novelist

Courage is almost a contradiction in terms. It means a strong desire to live taking the form of a readiness to die.

G. K. Chesterton
British author

We are not permitted to choose the frame of our destiny. But what we put into it is ours.

Dag Hammarskjöld
Swedish statesman

Hope, the patent medicine for disease, disaster, sin.

Wallace Rice
American poet

Great things are done when men and mountains meet; this is not done by jostling in the street.

Gnomic Verses

Heroism is the brilliant triumph of the soul over the flesh—that is to say, over fear: fear of poverty, of suffering, of calumny, of sickness, of isolation, and of death. There is no serious piety without heroism. Heroism is the dazzling and glorious concentration of courage.

Henri Frédéric Amiel
Swiss philosopher

She loved me for the dangers I had passed.

William Shakespeare
English playwright

'Tis true that we are in great danger; the greater therefore should our courage be.

William Shakespeare
English playwright

Cowards die many times before their deaths; the valiant never taste of death but once. Of all the wonders that I yet have heard, it seems to me most strange that men should fear, seeing that death, a necessary end will come when it will come.

William Shakespeare
English playwright

Ah, Hope! what would life be, stripped of thy encouraging smiles, that teach us to look behind the dark clouds of to-day, for the golden beams that are to gild the morrow.

Susanna Moodie
Canadian author

Unt'l the day of his death, no man can be sure of his courage.

Jean Anouilh
French playwright

Courage is not simply *one* of the virtues, but the form of every virtue at the testing point, which means at the point of highest reality.

C. S. Lewis
British writer

A gap is widening between the philosophy which says that man is morally responsible and the biological dictum that man is only a collection of past evolved adaptations. The biological position is gaining strength at such a rate that to keep up with current discoveries one must read the scientific journals daily.

Nevertheless, there is much left to understand, and one can reasonably argue that some of our behaviors are not determined by natural selection and genetic predispositions. These non-evolved traits are emergent responses, quirky activity of our cognitive apparatus, chance, chaos, and circumstances. They appear suddenly as a result of unusual gene combinations, never directly selected, but still biological. Theoretically, these traits give us the creativity to step beyond our evolution into unannounced vistas—new, novel, and strange. If any parts of it are genetic in origin, they also could be adaptive beyond the usual, offering new directions of natural selection.

Epilogue: The Depth of Our Knowledge

There are no two worlds, as C.P. Snow asserted—a scientific world and a much different historical world. The biology of today is the grand thoughts of yesterday—they flower together. Biology gives voice to our nature, as it investigates the origins and characteristics of our behavior. Literature unfolds that nature through insight and persistence. One is the other—too sides of the attempt to plum our being. Any cultural separation is simply arbitrary.

We are both propelled and constrained by our evolutionary history. That which we are interested in, and that which we think about, are, and can only be, mirrors of our evolution. Our ancestors carried the adaptations of survival and reproduction, those adaptations that regulate our behaviors today. How could we consider ourselves and our universe except through our own cognitive processes? We think like an Earthling, not a Martian; we see the world through the adaptations of the prehistoric savannah, not as objective machines. Even the machines we build are constructed according to our mental and physical dimensions.

What we say, how we say it, and what we do are expressions of our evolved traits. The implication is that the successful strategies for survival and reproduction are imprinted in our brain, available, at least in theory, to our consciousness. Any strategy that affected our behavior—any behavior that required mental effort—left its corollaries in the neural network of the brain. Thus, evolved strategies of love and sex, defense against outsiders, reactions to kin, deceptions and detection of cheaters, hope, fear, and all the rest, live on as ghosts within our brain. We see these things throughout history and in every culture.

None of this evolutionary knowledge is necessarily easy to call up into consciousness and examine. Mostly, genetic adaptations work effectively when they do not cause perturbations of the mind. Reflexive reaction is better than the conflict of self-reflection. My judgment is that behaviors have been selected for an *absence* of awareness. Awareness is strategic only when novelty confronts us, and when we must choose which evolutionary adaptation to apply.

It is in that moment of uncertainty that the mental ghosts of adaptation present themselves for self-examination, as in opening a file of past strategies. We choose, consciously or not, and move on. Even then, the ghosts pass quickly, leaving the slightest of traces. With luck the ghost shimmers long enough for analysis, occasioned, perhaps, by unusual circumstances, trauma, dreaming, or madness. The ghost assumes a momentary form that we recognize as the truth. If we are to make use of insights, one must isolate these moments, strip away the self-deception, and crystallize the truth.

Our recent relatives and contemporaries have done just that: they touch our evolutionary adaptations of the past and mold these into conscious thought and human language. Our good fortune, if deliverance from ignorance is our goal, is that unusual moments of awareness have left us a record of the truth. We read that record in myths, novels, philosophy and literature; we hear it in lectures, plays, and music; and we see it repeated in ourselves. We see that record in our analyses of all cultures. Our singular evolutionary track left only ancestors who shared the necessary adaptations that we call humanness. All others perished or failed to reproduce. We carry those adaptations; we carry the mental ghosts of evolution past.

In this brief book we have seen the intertwining of the biological sciences and thoughts of great and not-so-great men and women. Repeatedly, current science is illuminated by past written and verbal expression. As a result, biological sciences deal almost exclusively with concepts and feelings that stretch across our recorded history. Those traits that have always puzzled us, or haunted our moments of contemplation, are the same that propel modern biology.

Poets and philosophers, among many others, have long ago touched the essence of human nature. With genius and courage they constructed the relevant metaphors that helped generations understand themselves. We have witnessed their insights through quotations for nearly all important problems of human behavior. Certainly their grasp of the significant came before the development of systematic biology, and much of what they knew emerged before any formal study of human behavior, and even before naturalists considered the mechanisms of evolution. If one reads only backward from the achievements of biology, one is tempted to credit science with the only methodology leading to truth. But if one begins early, listening to the heart and soul of men and women expressing their own longings and uncertainties, one sees the road leading to the door of science. The remarkable achievements of today and tomorrow swing on the hinges of the past.

The past! the past! the past!
The past—the dark unfathom'd retrospect!
The teeming gulf—the sleepers and the shadows!
The past—the infinite greatness of the past!
For what is the present after all but a growth out of the past?

Walt Whitman

From the inevitable link between science and history we can draw together the threads of human nature in a way never before possible. Great thoughts abound, insights accumulate, and old ideas lie quietly. All these can be used as a new wave of biological study. Certainly we should mine everything from history, poetry, and literature for the nuggets of biological truths. They are there, just waiting to be picked up and refined.

Bibliography: References to Our Past

Introduction

Becker, E. (1973). *The denial of death*. New York: The Free Press.

Berger, R. (1977). *Psychosis*. San Francisco: W.H. Freeman and Company.

Piaget, J. (1970). Piaget's theory. In: P.H. Mussen (Ed.), *Carmichael's manual of child psychology*. (Vol. 1, 3rd Ed.). New York: John Wiley.

Snow, C.P. (1959). *The two cultures*. Cambridge: University of Cambridge Press.

Chapter 1: The Nature of Man

Becker, E. (1973). *The denial of death*. New York: The Free Press.

Darwin, C. (1871). *The descent of man*. Basic Books: Modern Library.

Dawkins, R. (1976). *The selfish gene*. New York: Oxford University Press.

Johanson, D., Johanson, L. & Edgar, B. (1994). *Ancestors: In search of human origins*. New York: Villard Books.

Liles, G. (1994). The faith of an atheist. *MD, 59–64*.

Lopreato, J. (1984). *Human nature and biocultural evolution*. Boston: Allen and Unwin.

Sarich, V.M. & Wilson, A.C. (1967). Immunological time scale for hominid evolution. *Science, 158*, 1200–1203.

Symons, D. (1992). On the use and misuse of Darwinism in the study of human behavior. In: J.H. Barkow, L. Cosmides and J. Tooby (Eds.), *The adapted mind: evolutionary psychology and the generation of culture*. New York: Oxford University Press, 137–159.

Tooby, J. & Cosmides, L. (1992). The psychological foundations of culture. In: J.H. Barkow, L. Cosmides and J. Tooby (Eds.), *The adapted mind: evolutionary psychology and the generation of culture*. New York: Oxford University Press, 19–136.

Wilson, E.O. (1975). *Sociobiology: A new synthesis*. Cambridge: Harvard University Press.

Chapter 2: Romantic Love, Passion, and the Price of Reproduction

Betzig, L. (1986). *Despotism and differential reproduction: A Darwinian view of history*. New York: Aldine de Gruyter.

Betzig, L. (1989). Causes of conjugal dissolution: A cross-cultural study. *Current Anthropology*, *30*, 654–676.

Buss, D.M. (1994). *The evolution of desire*. New York: Basic Books.

Buss, D.M., Larsen, R.J., Westen, D. and Semmelbroth, J. (1992). Sex differences in jealousy: Evolution, physiology, and psychology. *Psychological Science*, *3*, 251–255.

Ellis, L. (1995). Dominance and reproductive success among nonhuman animals: A cross-species comparison. *Ethology and Sociobiology*, In Press.

Fisher, H.E. (1992). *Anatomy of love: The natural history of monogamy, adultery, and divorce*. New York: Norton.

Jankowiak, W.R. and Fischer, E.F. (1992). A cross-cultural perspective on romantic love. *Ethology*, *31*, 149–155.

Johnston, V. and Franklin, M. (1993). Is beauty in the eye of the beholder? *Ethology and Sociobiology*, *14*, 183–200.

Pérusse, D. (1993). Cultural and reproductive success in industrial societies: Testing the relationship at the proximate and ultimate levels. *Behavioral and Brain Sciences*, 16, 267–284.

Rushton, P. (1995). *Race, evolution, and behavior*. New Brunswick, N.J.: Transaction Publishers.

Singh, D. (1993). Adaptive significance of waist-to-hip ratio and female physical attractiveness. *Journal of Personality and Social Psychology*, *65*, 293–307.

Thiessen, D.D. (1993). Environmental tracking by females: Sexual lability. *Human Nature*, *5*, 167–202.

Thiessen, D. and Gregg, B. (1980). Human assortative mating and genetic equilibrium: An evolutionary perspective. *Ethology and Sociobiology*, 1, 111–140.

Thornhill, R. (1993). The allure of symmetry. *Natural History*, 9, 31–36.

Trivers, R. (1972). Parental investment and sexual selection. In: B. Campbell (Ed.), *Sexual selection and the descent of man*. New York: Aldine de Gruyter, 136–179.

Chapter 3: The Dark Side of Human Nature

Brunner, H.G., Nelsen, M.R., van Zandvoort, P., Abeling, N.G.G.M., van Gennip, A.H., Wolters, E.C., Kulper, M.A., Ropers, H.H. and van Oost, B.A. (1993). X-linked borderline mental retardation with prominent behavioral disturbance: Phenotype, genetic localization, and evidence for disturbed monoamine metabolism. *American Journal of Human Genetics*, 52, 1032–1039.

Beck, A. (1994). Bureau of Justice Statistics. U.S. Department of Justice.

Dabbs, J.M., Jr. and Morris, R. (1990). Testosterone, social class, and antisocial behavior in a sample of 4,462 men. *Psychological Science*, *1*, 209–211.

Daly, M. and Wilson, M. (1981). Abuse and neglect of children in evolutionary perspective. In: R.D. Alexander and D.W. Tinkle (Eds.), *Natural selection and social behavior*. New York: Chiron Press, Inc., 405–416.

Daly, M. and Wilson, M. (1988). Evolutionary social psychology and family homicide. *Science, 242*, 519–524.

DiLalia, L.F. and Gottesman, I.I. (1991). Biological and genetic contributors to violence—Wisdom's untold tale. *Psychological Bulletin, 109*, 125–129.

Hare, R. (1993). *Without conscience: The disturbing world of the psychopaths among us*. New York: Simon and Schuster.

Herrnstein, R.J. and Murray, C. (1994). *The bell curve: Intelligence and class structure in American life*. New York: The Free Press.

Mednick, S.A., Gabrielli, W.F., Jr. and Hutchings, B. (1984). Genetic influences in criminal convictions: Evidence from an adoption cohort. *Science, 224*, 891–894.

Reiss, A.J. and Roth, J.A. (Eds.) (1993). *Understanding and preventing violence*. Washington, D.C.: National Academy Press.

Sheets-Johnstone, M. (1990). The roots of thinking. Philadelphia: Temple University Press.

Straus, M.A. and Gelles, R.J. (1990). Physical violence in American families: Risk factors and adaptations to violence in 8,145 families. New Brunswick, N.J.: Transaction Publishers.

Thiessen, D. (1996). *Bitter-sweet destiny: The stormy evolution of human behavior*. New Brunswick, N.J.: Transaction Publishers.

Wilson, J.Q. and Hernstein, R.J. (1985). *Crime and human nature*. New York: Simon and Schuster.

Chapter 4: The Duality of the Human Brain

Calvin, W.H. (1990). *The ascent of mind*. New York: Bantam Books.

Crick, F. (1994). *The astonishing hypothesis: The scientific search for the soul*. New York: Charles Scribner's Sons.

Eccles, J.C. (1989). *Evolution of the brain: Creation of the self*. London: Routledge.

Jerison, H.J. (1985). Animal intelligence as encephalization. *Philosophical Transactions of the Royal Society of London B., 308*, 21–35.

Johanson, D. and Johanson, L. (1994). *Ancestors: In search of human origins*. New York: Villard Books.

Leakey, R. and Lewin, R. (1992). *Origins: Reconsidered*. New York: Doubleday.

MacLean, P.D. (1970). The triune brain, emotion, and scientific bias. In: F.O. Schmitt (Ed.), *The neurosciences, second study program*. New York: The Rockefeller University Press, 336–349.

MacNeilage, P.F. (in press). Prolegomena to a theory of the sound pattern of the first spoken language. *Phonetica*.

Piaget, J. (1970). Piaget's theory. In: P.H. Mussen (Ed.), *Carmichael's manual of child psychology*. (Vol 1, 3rd Ed.). New York: John Wiley.

Posner, M.I. and Rothbart, M.K. (1994). Constructing neuronal theories of mind. In: K. Christof and Davis, J.L. (Eds.), *Large-scale neuronal theories of the brain*. Cambridge: The MIT Press, 183–199.

Vrba, E.S. (1985). Environment and evolution: Alternative causes of the temporal distribution of evolutionary events. *South African Journal of Science*, 81, 229–236.

Chapter 5: The Historical Depth of Culture

Alexander, R.D. (1979). *Darwinism and human affairs*. Seattle: University of Washington Press.

Barash, D.P. (1977). *Sociobiology and behavior*. New York: Elsevier.

Brown, D.E. (1991). *Human universals*. Philadelphia: Temple University Press.

Dawkins, R. (1976). *The selfish gene*. Oxford: Oxford University Press.

Dawkins, R. (1995). *River out of Eden*. New York: Basic Books.

Thiessen, D. (1996). *Bitter-sweet destiny: The stormy evolution of human behavior*. New Brunswick, N.J.: Transaction Publishers.

Tooby, J. and Cosmides, L. (1992). The psychological foundations of culture. In: J.H. Barkow, L. Cosmides and J. Tooby (Eds.), *The adapted mind*. New York: Oxford University Press, 19–136.

Trivers, R. (1972). Parental investment and sexual selection. In: B. Campbell (Ed.), *Sexual selection and the descent of man*. New York: Aldine de Gruyter, 136–179.

Wilson, E.O. (1975). *Sociobiology: A new synthesis*. Cambridge: Harvard University Press.

Chapter 6: Creativity and the Pains of Deviation

Cohen, D.B. (1994). *Out of the blue*. New York: W.W. Norton and Company.

Ewald, P.W. (1994). *Evolution of infectious disease*. Oxford: Oxford University Press.

Jamison, K.R. (1995). Manic-depressive illness and creativity. *Scientific American*, 272, 62–67.

Nesse, R.M. and Williams, G.C. (1994). *Why we get sick*. New York: Times Books.

Chapter 7: Masters of Death

Asprey, R.B. (1994). *War in the shadows: The guerrilla in history*. New York: William Morrow and Company, Inc.

Clausewitz, C. (1976). *On war*. (M. Howard and P. Pared, Eds.), Princeton, N.J.: Princeton University Press.

Daly, M. and Wilson, M. (1988). *Homicide*. New York: Aldine de Gruyter.

Diamond, J. (1992). *The third chimpanzee: The evolution and future of the human animal*. New York: Harper Perennial.

Green, P.A. (1991). A biocultural analysis of revolution. *Journal of Social and Biological Structures, 14*, 435–454.

Lopreato, J. and Green, F.P.A. (1990). The evolutionary foundations of revolution. In: J. van der Dennen, and V. Falger (Eds.), *Sociobiology and conflict*. London: Chapman and Hall, 107–122.

Thiessen, D. (1996). *Bitter-sweet destiny: The stormy evolution of human behavior*. New Brunswick, N.J.: Transaction Publishers.

Van Creveld, M. (1991). *The transformation of war*. New York: The Free Press.

Weatherford, J. (1994). *Savages and civilization*. New York: Crown Publishers.

Chapter 8: Trying to Go Beyond the Genes

Dawkins, R. (1986). *The blind watchmaker*. Harlow: Longman.

Gleick, J. (1987). *Chaos: Making a new science*. New York: Viding Penguin, Incorporated.

Gould, S.J. (1989). *Wonderful life*. New York: W. W. Norton and Company.

Gutzwiller, M.C. (1992). Quantum chaos. *Scientific American, 266*, 78–84.

Lewin, R. (1992). *Complexity: Life at the edge of chaos*. New York: Macmillan Publishing Company.

Lykken, D.T., McGue, M., Telligen, A. and Bouchard, T.J., Jr. (1992). Emergenesis: Genetic traits that may not run in families. *American Psychologist, 47*, 1565– 1577.

Prigogine, I. and Stengers, O. (1984). *Order out of chaos: Man's new dialogue with nature*. Toronto: Bantam Books.

Swinney, H.L. (1993). Predictability and chaos. *Discovery, 13*, 27–31.

Thiessen, D. (1996). *Bitter-sweet destiny: The stormy evolution of human behavior*. New Brunswick, N.J.: Transaction Publishers.

Index